WHAT I WISH I'D KNOWN ABOUT

RAISING A CHILD
with autism

A MOM *and a* PSYCHOLOGIST
OFFER HEARTFELT GUIDANCE
for the FIRST FIVE YEARS

BOBBI SHEAHAN AND
KATHY DeORNELLAS, PH.D.

FUTURE HORIZONS INC.
Arlington, Texas

What I Wish I'd Known About
Raising a Child with Autism

All marketing and publishing rights guaranteed to and reserved by:

FUTURE HORIZONS INC.

721 W. Abram Street
Arlington, Texas 76013
800-489-0727
817-277-0727
817-277-2270 (fax)
E-MAIL: *info@FHautism.com*
www.FHautism.com

Book design © TLC Graphics, *www.TLCGraphics.com*
Cover by: Tamara Dever; Interior by: Erin Stark

Publisher's Cataloging-In-Publication Data
(Prepared by The Donohue Group, Inc.)

Sheahan, Bobbi Reilly.

   What I wish I'd known about raising a child with autism / Bobbi Sheahan and Kathy DeOrnellas.

      p. ; cm.

   Includes bibliographical references and index.
   ISBN: 978-1-935274-23-0

   1. Parents of autistic children--Popular works. 2. Autistic children—Psychology—Popular works. 3. Autism in children—Popular works. 4. Parenting—Popular works. I. DeOrnellas, Kathy. II. Title.

RJ506.A9 S54 2011
618.92/858/82

Printed in Canada

... and a little child shall lead them.

— Isaiah 11:6

Dedication

To my daughter and my husband,
for bringing me to your planet to live,

And to Dr. DeOrnellas for being my tour guide.

To paraphrase A. A. Milne,
This would be my gift to you if it weren't your gift to me.

— B. S.

To my husband Ron for making it possible for me to
drop everything else and write this book,
and to my daughter, Erin, for all your support.
Together, you make my life possible.

— K. D.

Acknowledgements

Of course, I'll start with my family. Ben, you are my life. Thanks for believing in me and taking over bedtime with the kids so that I could write. And to my kids, it is never a dull moment! I love you with my every breath.

Dr. Kathy DeOrnellas, for believing in me, my kid, my family, my sanity, this book, I am forever in your debt. Not everyone is lucky enough to bring their child to you; it is my privilege to share you with the world. I also need to thank your husband for putting up with our writing schedule.

To Erin, Sondi, and Dylan Tran, for believing in us and helping us, often in the wee hours.

Kelly Gilpin, how do I start to thank you? Thank you for fighting for our book. Everyone should have an advocate like you. Thanks to Tamara Dever for the amazing cover design, and to Erin Stark for making our words look so good, and to our entire team at Future Horizons.

Thank you, Tamy Lindemeyer, for being the brave friend who gently pointed me in the direction of help. Did you ever know what that has meant for me? Now you do.

To the brave and candid parents who answered my survey, thank you and thank your children.

To Elizabeth Scott and David H. Albert for your kindness, your wisdom, and your encouragement.

Thanks, Mario Dovile and Chris Buechler for fixing our house so many times. (We're not done.)

To the Marks, Moos, Reisinger, Valdivia, Lozano, and Dostalik families, thank you for embracing our family and sharing yours with us.

For loving us enough to not be afraid of me and my kids, I thank Morgan Whatley; Heather Nevitt; Andrea Todd; Franci McFarland; Sara and Rick Meyer (with a special shout-out to Joe); Dr. Dane and Sapna Fleidner; Janet and Ruth Rickert; Evelyn Greenberg; Donna and Chris Maxwell; Jennifer Zerangue; Art and Karen Reilly; Dan and Sheena Reilly; Dr. Arnett and Nikki Klugh; Dr. Doug and Kathleen MacKinnon; Dr. Justin and Michelle Yang; Dr. HoeYel Cho, Jenogae Mun, and Haelin Cho; Dr. Mike Flynn and Dr. Linda Sattler Flynn; Dr. Malini Hebbur, Loyette Stewart, and the lovely Nurses Patti and Debbie; Fr. Loyd Morris; Fran Morris; Elizabeth and Natasha Varughese; Allison Adams, Taylor and Phaedra Johnson, Angela Roach, Veronica Kellmeyer; Heather King, Fara Goldsmith, Anita Walker, Grace and Kayli LeBlanc; Sara Akers; Kendra, Monica, and Armando Lara; Dave and Alanna De La Garza; Irfan Chaudry and Dr. Fatima Maqbool; Fr. Paul Weinberger; Vina and Christine Kaczmarczyk; Ann Waldyn; all of my marvelous in-laws, and my parents, Art and Dolly Reilly. Each of you has touched my life in ways for which I cannot adequately thank you.

Father Jason Cargo, thank you for reminding me that my children are here as instruments of God's grace in my life. May I be the same to them.

Charles Fletcher, Bailey Gramling, Gracie, Ziggy, and the entire staff—both two-legged and four-legged—at Spirit Horse. You are a blessing that autism has brought into our lives.

To Mr. Matt, who reached out to my daughter and told her that it's ok to be different. Thanks.

I saved the most important acknowledgement for last: thank you, God, my Father, who made us all exactly the way we are, on purpose and for a purpose.

Table of Contents

Preface

Why Did We Write This Book, and Why Do You Need to Read It?

Let's start with the "who" part, which will tell you "why" as well: I (Bobbi) am a parent who teamed up with an autism professional to spare other parents the pain, confusion, and discouragement that I went through in the initial stages of discovering that my daughter had an autism spectrum disorder. Cutting through the confusion and getting a diagnosis was much harder than actually dealing with the difficulties themselves. We'd like to spare you some of that if we can.

Although I am a natural know-it-all, I'm not here to give you a diagnosis or to tell you how to parent; instead, think of this book as a scouting report. *What I Wish I'd Known about Raising a Child with Autism* was written during the first seven years of parenting my daughter Grace, with a focus on the first four years. Grace lives with an autism spectrum disorder (we'll sometimes refer to it as an ASD). As you have probably already figured out, every child is different, and that is especially true of kids on the autism spectrum. For example, Grace's sensory issues were, and continue to be, extreme. As for the verbal challenges and eye contact, while Grace's challenges were daunting at first, we have seen amazing improvement. Then there are other areas, like social functioning, the differences in the way she thinks, and developmental delays, in which every day is a new and different experience. Both before and after finding Dr. DeOrnellas and getting a diagnosis for Grace, my husband and I looked under every rock and considered a wide range of possible diagnoses and prognoses.

The first signs of autism can be confusing—not to mention scary. Maybe our book will help you learn where to start to look for answers. Or perhaps someone has given this book to you so that you can better understand your student, grandchild, or patient. However you came to us, you are welcome here. We are here to talk about some really hard truths, and we aren't here to judge you or your kid.

Like our children, this book is unique. There are many informative books to help you with specific problems that you may encounter; we tell you about some of the best of these books. We are here to hold your hand as you walk through a door that you and your child didn't choose; come on in, there are lots of us here waiting for you. Maybe we can help you to figure out whether what you are seeing is (or could be) an autism spectrum disorder; maybe we can point you in the right direction for more help.

What I Wish I'd Known about Raising a Child with Autism is our love letter to Grace and our gift to the wave of parents who come behind us; it is our way to help you get on with the formidable tasks and great joys that you face. You may feel alone, but you aren't. Current estimates place around 1 in 100 kids on the autism spectrum, and the numbers are even higher among boys. When we were growing up, the numbers were more like 1 in several thousand.

You (probably) aren't losing your mind, although you may feel like it. Such feelings are a reasonable response to an explosion like this, especially when that explosion is taking place inside your child's brain. Let's start to make some sense of this. I'll dive right in by telling you about my Grace.

Authors' Note

We have changed or obscured some identifying details of people who did not volunteer to be in this book, and even some who did, like Bobbi's kids. We are eternally grateful to the generous people who provided insights and quotes for the book, and we have protected their privacy while accurately quoting them and/or telling their truth, as best as we could.

CHAPTER ONE

Our Journey from Cluelessness to Partial Enlightenment

I didn't set out to write a book. I only wanted to help my child.

Our story starts in early 2005. We were beginning the paperwork for an adoption. What kind of baby would we bring home? It seemed strange to us that we could specify our child's gender, health, or anything else, since our first two children had emerged from my body with no questionnaires or checklists.

Our first child, Lucy, was the classic high-maintenance toddler. She had embraced the Terrible Twos and the Disney princesses at the same time, with often-hilarious results. She was very demanding, very verbal, she ate everything that we gave her, and she was a happy, funny kid. She took her naps on a schedule and went through an unfortunate biting binge just before her second birthday. She was, in other words, a totally terrific, totally beautiful little girl.

Her sister Grace, born fifteen months later, was, in our opinion, the sweetest baby ever born. This pregnancy had been medically complicated, and even more harrowing and miserable than my first pregnancy, which was no picnic. Grace's birth and infancy were as easy as the pregnancy had been difficult. Grace looked like a porcelain doll. She rarely cried, and her vocalizations sounded like the meows of a little cat. She loved to be cuddled and squeezed. We thought it was a little odd that she never wanted to take a nap and that she didn't cry when she got her shots, but we didn't think it was a big deal. She didn't embrace solid food unless it was sweet, smooth, and room temperature, but we weaned her shortly after her first birthday and doggedly kept introducing new foods, most of which she rejected. Other than jaundice at birth and a bout with croup when she was a year old, she was robustly healthy. She skipped crawling, went straight to walking, and was running, climbing, tipping over other toddlers, and generally wreaking havoc by her first birthday. We were very much enjoying our two children and looking forward to a third.

It's funny how you look back at conversations that seemed so insignificant at the time. "Honey, I met this woman who has a ten-year-old son, and she told me the most bizarre, awful story," I related breathlessly. "She had the exact same pregnancy complications that I had with Grace, only her son was born with something called Asperger's syndrome." He hadn't heard of it either. I went on to regale him with the story of the woman's son grabbing her ponytail and bashing her head against the bathtub faucet because the temperature of his bath wasn't to his liking. "Their other kids aren't like this. This thing that he has, it makes it so he doesn't understand that he's hurting his mom. Can you imagine?" Years would pass before I gave that conversation another serious thought.

Meanwhile, Grace's second birthday came and went and she hadn't said a single word. She still meowed, with no babbling or consonant sounds. We joked that her sister, whose first word had been "happy" sometime around nine months, was her spokesperson and she simply saw no need to chat. It certainly was understandable that a person could have trouble getting a word in edgewise in our very verbal household! We mentioned this, along with her high pain tolerance, to her pediatrician at her well-child visits. She didn't seem worried. One friend had already gingerly suggested that Grace might have "sensory sensitivities" like one of her children. Moms at the park were starting to comment on her lack of eye contact and on the way that she walked the perimeter of the playground instead of interacting with the other children. A stranger, who had been in her presence for half an hour, told me with confidence that Grace was Just Like Her Son, who had been diagnosed with PDD-NOS. PD-what? I had no idea what that was; I'd never heard of it. I took umbrage at the suggestion that there was something "wrong" with my child and chalked it up to another hyper-vigilant parent running every trap to ensure that her child was Of High Quality, jumping on a fad, and seeking validation from a stranger at the park. Then it happened again. And again.

Around this time, my book club read a novel titled *The Curious Incident of the Dog in the Night-Time,* and I thought that it was absolutely fascinating. I'd never considered what it was like to be autistic, and I thought, "How odd. How interesting. How weird." Of course, it had *nothing* to do with me. Again, it's one of those things that make me, in retrospect, say "Duh," but I was without a clue at the time.

Meanwhile, the wheels of our adoption process ground on inexorably. We filled out checklists about what kinds of special needs we'd consider. Mostly we said No, we're not medical professionals. No, we have two small kids already and we don't want a medical odyssey, just a child to embrace and love. No, we wouldn't know how to help a child with special needs. What kind of saints would *ask* for a child with special needs? Well, maybe some *really little* special needs ... I mean, nothing *too* special. How naïve we were! How crass it felt to presume to say what we were willing to take on! I often agonized and thought, "This is a human being we're talking about!" It felt like shopping: Yes, I'll have the blue sweater, but not the one with the yellow buttons ... sigh. Certainly, we wouldn't volunteer for a child with neurological issues. What in the world did we know about those? How would we be competent to deal with THAT?

Meanwhile, Grace moved through her third year without showing the slightest inclination towards potty training. This baffled me, since her older sister had been fastidious and eager to please and I had wondered why parents made such a big deal of it. In fact, around this time, I ignorantly observed to my husband's best friend The Shocking Fact That Some Boys in Kindergarten Still Wear Pull Ups! And what a scandal was THAT? He refrained from slapping me and patiently explained that yes, his son was among the one-third or so of boys whose bladders just weren't ready for full-time man-pants just yet. I was mortified. It was a lesson—unfortunately not my last—in not judging other people's kids. Or their parenting.

As 2006 turned into 2007, things just got curiouser and curiouser with Grace. She would freak out if her sister changed the words when singing a favorite song, and she showed little interest in making friends. One bright spot was her lovely relationship with Miguel, a child who had been diagnosed with autism. Grace not only sought him out, but joined him in his world. My patient husband spent endless hours pushing the two of them on the swings. Grace even held Miguel's hand. In fact, she was one of the few people whose touch he tolerated. When he barked, she barked back. Fools that we were, we said things like, "What a precious child we have! She is reaching out to him! Maybe one day she'll work with kids with special needs." It seriously never crossed our mind that *she recognized one of her own tribe and was simply comfortable with him.* I mean, we were starting to learn about autism, but didn't that happen only to *boys*?

Between the ages of two and three, Grace began speaking. Her words came out in bursts that made us think that she was a precocious talker. While other children sounded out words and memorized nursery rhymes, she memorized poems, chapters, pages of dialogue, all seven dwarves and all twelve days of Christmas. She would parrot them in the most incongruous way, but we didn't immediately appreciate that *she had no idea what she was actually saying.* She would imitate accents, inflections, and sounds perfectly. Brilliant parents that we were, we thought it was kind of cool. It was past her third birthday before we began to realize that it was our baby speaking, but that we weren't really hearing her *voice.*

She was mechanically precocious, too. We have blazed new trails in childproofing. Lack of fear and the ability to defeat locks are a potent combination. She would do things like climb on top of our shelving, our minivan, or our refrigerator if I turned my back for a second. I began taking her *everywhere* with me (use your imagination—on second thought, no, don't) just for her own safety. Well, that and my sanity. She was also trashing our house. Our handyman was amazed—and enriched—by the things that she was able to break and the way that she was able to break them. While some degree of this kind of behavior is normal for small children, it persisted with increasing sophistication and no signs of stopping.

She took risks we couldn't understand. I have to tell you about the light bulbs. There was the time she grabbed a hot light bulb and burned the skin off of her hand. I screamed and yanked her hand off the lamp. Instead of responding to her burned palm, she put her hands over her ears with an anguished look. After one memorable incident, I learned not to put her into her room alone for a nap. (Not that she **ever** slept during the day, but I did need a break, and so did she.) Grace had long since laid waste to all of our floor lamps. There was nothing in Grace's room except her bed, a bookshelf that was bolted to the wall, and a light fixture protruding from the wall more than five feet off of the floor, far out of her reach. (So we thought.) I heard a crash and thought, "Dang it, she's climbed on that bookshelf again, I guess I'll have to take that out too," but I opened the door to find Grace lying on top of a pile of books (which was not an unusual sight) with a big grin on her face. She was crunching on something and there was blood spattered on the books and on her pillow. In a fraction of a second, my mind raced: *there's nothing crunchy in here and where did that blood*

5

come from? Oh-no-the-light-fixture's-down-and-holy-moley-it's-the-light-bulb! She cheerfully spat out the glass on command.

The veteran doctor who examined her told me that he assumed that the blood came only from her hands and that I should watch her stools for blood.

That's it? No tests?

"Well, I can do whatever kind of scan you want, but glass isn't going to show up," he said. "She's not in distress, there are no cuts in her mouth, her heart isn't racing, she's able to speak, she's breathing fine, so the likelihood is that she didn't swallow any glass. If you see blood in her diaper, call me on the way to the emergency room. Better yet, call an ambulance first, then call me." I was baffled and panicky. I asked something stupid like, "Is there anything in particular I should feed her, or avoid feeding her? "Yeah," he replied. "Avoid red food."

Speaking of red, there was the time that any other child would have noticed that she was standing on an anthill and dozens of fire ants were biting her legs. She looked like her legs were covered in sprinkles. Sprinkles that moved. Sprinkles that bit. By the time I stopped screaming and hosed them all off, she had over forty bites. Not only did she never complain about the pain, but I had to drag her away from multiple anthills in the months that followed.

Grace would also throw herself down on the ground for no apparent reason. Twice before she turned four, she needed stitches to her face, and she never cried—at least not from the pain. The ER sure did freak her out, though.

As Grace's vocabulary increased, so did her speech, but she seemed not to understand the meaning of what she was saying or, for that matter, what others were saying. She sometimes took an inordinate amount of time processing someone else's speech or formulating her own. She was not able to participate in adult-directed activities, no matter how direct or brief. Whether it was the organized games at a three-year-old's birthday party or swim lessons, she was totally tuned out.

Meanwhile, it seemed to me that the professionals were trying hard to convince everyone around me that their kids had an "autism spectrum disorder," something I'd heard of in passing back in a psych class in college. Actually, nobody mentioned a spectrum back in the 1980s; I recall a single passing reference to autism as "childhood schizophrenia," characterizing the autistic as "locked fortresses," whose condition was caused by "refrigerator mothers." Obviously, that had nothing to do with the wonderful kids and parents I knew. Why make a big deal if Junior doesn't want to participate in freakin' circle time? He's only three, for goodness' sake! Why didn't parents trust themselves and let nature take its course, I wondered. In the '90s, it was ADHD. Now, everyone was talking about sensory differences, the autism spectrum, and speech therapy. "What does that preschool teacher know?" I demanded of my friend. "There's not a thing wrong with your son; he's perfect. If my sweet little petunia were in that preschool, they'd be trying to shrink her head too! What's wrong with being a little shy, a little accident-prone?" I shrieked to more than one friend. "While we're at it, why is every three-year-old boy I know in speech therapy?"

Again, duh. Sometimes being reasonably bright and independent works against you. We don't like to think of ourselves as slow on the uptake, but it took another problem to make us realize that we were looking at something we simply didn't understand. In the summer and fall of 2007, our mellow little girl began making unprovoked attacks on other children. She would bite them, slam them to the ground, or pull out handfuls of their hair, then be mystified that they didn't want to play with her. She would also break things—lots of things. She never seemed upset when she was being aggressive. Her lack of emotional response to these incidents—and her lack of understanding of other people's responses—made no sense to us at all. It took us a long time to realize that she was reciting dialogue and playing out scenes from books and videos, and that she didn't actually intend to hurt anyone or even really understand what she was doing. I just didn't get it. How could she fail to see that body-slamming isn't fun, especially when the slam-ee is *clearly* upset, terrified, and angry?

We were losing friends. Then we lost a babysitter. Nobody understood why Grace did the things she did. We'd be holding her hand in a parking lot and she'd wrench away and run towards danger. You might expect this from a two-year-old, but Grace wasn't two anymore. We were confused. How could someone so agile be so accident-prone? Why did she seem oblivious to the sound of our voices, yet scream in terror and pain when I turned on the blender? And speaking of pain, why didn't she feel pain when she was obviously hurt? We ruled out hearing problems. We wondered where to turn.

I went back to my pediatrician in desperation. She gave me a list of psychologists and encouraged me to get as many opinions as I needed. As I began to call down the list—and to expand on it—I was stunned. While many, many folks were generous with their time and helped me to narrow down the possible diagnoses (mercifully eliminating a lot of other, scarier, possible explanations for her behavior), I had a terrible time finding someone willing to even evaluate a three-year-old. (In the small number of years since the events I've described here, the psychological and educational communities have made impressive strides towards understanding the importance of early detection and early intervention for kids with autism. I applaud this; I only wish that had been the case when Grace was three.) When I called the insurance company, the woman on the phone was initially surprised that I'd be looking for a psychologist for a three-year-old. By the time I got done telling the story I've related here, she not only pre-approved sessions with three different professionals (I had found exactly three psychologists in a hundred-mile radius who were willing to evaluate a three-year-old), but she also volunteered that she had pre-approved counseling for the other members of our family if we needed it, stating that she expected that it would be very stressful to cope with these kinds of challenges, and we might need someone to talk to.

When an insurance company volunteers to give you money, it gets your attention.

Luckily for us—and I don't really believe in luck—the second psychologist to whom we spoke was the lovely, the talented, the amazing Dr. Kathy DeOrnellas. She didn't judge us, she didn't insult us, and she amazed us up front by telling us that kids with Asperger's were some of her favorite people. By this point in our journey, this level of kindness and empathy came as a bit of a shock. Before Dr. DeOrnellas became my co-author, she rescued my child from her silence and helped us learn how to reach her.

Believe me, we appreciated the help. There were things we did that were stupid, like thinking that the doll that pee-pees was going to teach her on the ninth time around. There were also things that we did right without realizing it, like not putting Grace in a group daycare and eliminating television (I was tired of hearing her parrot entire episodes of cartoons, and now we skip TV and monitor the content of occasional videos instead). We also had a steep learning curve regarding the violent content in media, even in such innocuous things as Bible stories. When Grace acted things out, she was literal, whether that meant creating art in ways that you wouldn't anticipate (she destroyed four beds before her fourth birthday), or whacking a friend with a brick ("But he SAID he was a rock giant!" was her wide-eyed defense as he bled and cried).

There have been unexpected blessings along the way. When Grace's sister joined the family, we were suddenly thankful for the fact that Grace was a bit oblivious to social cues and pain. For the first few weeks that Mary was home, she was outraged by the existence of a sister close in age who expected to sit on Mommy's lap. *Ever.* While we had been concerned that Grace might be aggressive towards Mary, we needn't have worried. It was the other way around. Twenty-month-old Mary's first word to Grace was "Dop!" accompanied by a slap to the face as Grace tried to hug me. Mary bit her, hit her, and generally rejected her. Grace, being Grace, was confused by this behavior, rather than upset. Since we were already teaching Grace things by endless, patient repetition at this point, I spent a lot of time showing her how to win Mary over with toys and snacks. (I also had some guidance for Mary, but that's a whole 'nother book.) Over the next months, I witnessed Grace's kindness and patience in a totally new light. Before long, the two had developed a sibling relationship, in every sense of the word. (But if you're conjuring up a picture of them skipping through the meadow hand in hand and sharing the cookies without complaint, that's only an accurate picture every third Tuesday, for a few minutes.)

As one problem recedes, another one—sometimes a totally new one—takes center stage. Take the sudden proclivity to eat non-food items. We learned that this disorder, known as *pica,* is common among kids with autism spectrum disorders. Small disruptions to her routine can rock her world as though she's being evacuated for a hurricane. When Grace began speaking more normally and making eye contact, her uncanny ability to memorize chunks of text seemed to fade. Yet her memory still surprises me. On the way to a parade, for example, she became upset and repeatedly insisted, "I need to wear my Pocahontas costume!" Although we hadn't discussed it in 364 days, she remembered vividly what she had worn the previous year when we had been on a float in the parade. She will sometimes fail to acknowledge a question, but then literally pick up the conversation months later. "I remember the first time I met Mr. Meyer. I told him I was sorry for whacking Joe with a brick," she said, apropos of nothing, several months after the fact.

We understand new things every day. For some months when she was three, I could avoid the Sunday Walk of Shame if I wore a certain dress to church. The textured pattern of the fabric was very soothing and fascinating to Grace. I was really glad when that phase passed. The dress was the color of a sports drink.

I now know that when Grace is around other kids for any length of time, especially if this takes place away from home, she is going to need serious downtime—sometimes days of it. When she is anxious, she wants to be squeezed much more tightly than I would find comfortable. If we make the slightest change to her room, she will grieve wildly. We've learned not to let her delays in communication or maturity fool us about the fact that she is very, very intelligent.

Now, it seems presumptuous to write a book when we're so early into our journey, but I want to share the lessons we've learned—some at a painful cost—to comfort and encourage those who come behind us. I needed to do it while it was fresh in my heart and mind. I wish that such a book had existed for me. The first years of a parent's journey with a child like ours can be lonely and confusing. For every leap of progress, there seems to be a price in another area, and sometimes a trip to the grocery store feels like an exercise in ritual humiliation. There are the days when I just want to give up, but then someone who hasn't seen Grace for a while says, "Wow! She's come so far, it's hard to believe I'm looking at the same kid!"

As of this writing, Grace's diagnosis is PDD-NOS (Pervasive Developmental Disorder, Not Otherwise Specified). Allow me to digress into a little explanation of what I barely understand. PDD-NOS means autism. In lay terms, Grace's diagnosis places us smack in the middle of the fluctuating autism spectrum, between Asperger's syndrome and frank autism (also known as Kanner autism, classic autism, or profound autism—these are the kids who are the least verbal and have the highest degree of the behaviors and challenges described in this book). Actually, in our case, Grace can literally cover the whole spectrum in the course of a day. You may notice that Asperger's syndrome is sometimes referred to as Asperger syndrome or Asperger's disorder. Somewhere, professionals are arguing about this even as we speak. You may also notice that I sound more like a mom than a professional when I try to describe the technical terms; I'll leave that to Dr. DeOrnellas. Frankly, the name that they give to my baby's diagnosis doesn't really matter to anyone except the insurance company. All I can do is to tell you our story and what I've learned, and hope that it will light your path in some small way. Since I can't come to your house and bring you to Dr. DeOrnellas' office—and believe me, I would if I could—I'm bringing her to you.

Like everything else, now that I'm aware, I see it everywhere. From the socially inept teenager who wants to talk endlessly about the tax code to the three-year-old who won't take direction, chafes at her "scratchy" diapers, and walks on tiptoe, I can't help seeing the hallmarks of autism everywhere I look, now that my eyes have been opened.

If you're reading this book, it's likely that the worst is already behind you. You've already dreamed up nightmare scenarios about your child's condition and prognosis and begun grieving the imaginary family you thought you'd have. If you are a parent of a child who is quirky, you may feel you're a member of a club that you never volunteered to join. Maybe some of you will see your own children in these pages and be spared the feeling that you're trying to connect the dots with a blindfold on. Maybe we can reduce the isolation and break the silence just a little bit. The fact that you're reading this book means that you've started to mobilize, even if you aren't done grieving. It does get easier. I wish I could tell you that it gets better from here. Well, sometimes it does. Except when it gets worse. Okay, maybe even a lot worse. And then better again. At least Dr. DeOrnellas and I can help you figure out what the hell is going on.

CHAPTER TWO

Autism 101

By Kathy DeOrnellas, Ph.D.

As Bobbi mentioned earlier, autism spectrum disorders (ASDs), or Pervasive Developmental Disorders, are the fastest growing class of developmental disabilities in the United States and currently affect over 1.5 million Americans (Autism Society of America [ASA]). In December, 2009, the Centers for Disease Control and Prevention issued a report concluding that the prevalence of autism had risen to one in every 110 births (up from previous estimates of one in 150) in the United States and to almost one in seventy boys (up from one in every ninety-four in 2007). Also in 2007, representatives for the National Survey of Children's Health (NSCH) spoke with the parents or guardians of over 100,000 children in the U.S. and determined that one in ninety-one children aged three to seventeen had a current diagnosis. Many of the parents who were surveyed reported that their child had initially been diagnosed with autism, but no longer carried that diagnosis. One possible explanation for this is that their child participated in an early childhood screening and was suspected of having autism; however, the diagnosis of autism was eventually ruled out and the child was either given a different diagnosis, or no diagnosis was warranted as the child matured.

The phenomenal rise in autism diagnoses has been widely discussed on television and in the press (Cowley, 2003). Despite the vast amount of research being conducted each year, we still do not know for sure what causes autism or why it is increasing at such an alarming rate. We are beginning to understand the toll that it can take on families, school systems, and communities. The ASA (2009) estimates that it costs $3.5 to $5 million to care for a child with autism over his lifetime; the United States spends almost $90 billion each year for autism. This figure includes research, health care, education, housing, transportation, etc. It has been seventy years since Kanner first wrote about children with autism, and Asperger wrote about children with a higher functioning form of autism (now called Asperger's syndrome). Since that time, we have learned a great deal; however, we still have far to go.

Although I will frequently refer to "children with ASDs" it is important to remember that autism is a life-long disorder. Children do not outgrow it although their behaviors may change over time or improve in some ways. Adolescents and adults have ASD and it can affect their lives just as severely as it can for children.

ASDs, also known as Pervasive Developmental Disorders, are diagnosed by comparing a child's behavior (or the behavior of an individual at any age) to a set of symptoms that have been established as the diagnostic criteria. In the United States, the *Diagnostic and Statistical Manual of Mental Disorders-Fourth Edition-Text Revision (DSM-IV-TR*; American Psychiatric Association, 2000) is the most widely used set of symptoms. The *DSM-IV-TR* is a sort of encyclopedia of mental health disorders. Psychiatrists write the *DSM-IV-TR* and use a medical model for interpreting behavioral symptoms of mental health problems. This is the fourth edition of the *Diagnostic and Statistical Manual of Mental Disorders* and the diagnosis of autism has been handled differently in each edition.

As we learn more about a disorder, changes are made in the diagnostic criteria.

Although it is used in some countries outside the U.S., you may also read about the *ICD-10*. The *ICD-10* is the tenth edition of the *International Classification of Diseases*, which is published by the World Health Organization. Since autism is diagnosed in individuals all over the world, it is important to recognize that the *DSM-IV-TR* is not the only tool used for diagnosing individuals.

Characteristics of Children with Autism Spectrum Disorders

In order to understand individuals with ASDs better, it is important to recognize the features of the disorders that fall under the umbrella known as Pervasive Developmental Disorders. In this book we will refer to them as ASDs. Several types of ASDs have been identified and it is most helpful to think of them as falling on a continuum. Autism is at one end of the continuum and is the most severe type of ASD. Children with autism have unusual behaviors that are repetitive and stereotypical, as well as very restricted interests and activities. They have severely disordered verbal and nonverbal language and as many as half of them never develop any type of language. Autism is also characterized by impairments in social interaction that include poor eye-to-eye gaze, lack of social or emotional turn taking, and a failure to develop relationships with peers. The play of children with autism lacks imagination and creativity. Most children with autism also have delayed intellectual abilities (*DSM-IV-TR*, 2000). Autism appears four to five times more often in males than females; however, females with autism are more likely to be severely mentally retarded (*DSM-IV-TR*).

On the other end of the autism spectrum or continuum, children with Asperger's disorder generally have age-appropriate expressive and receptive language skills and average intelligence or above. They have difficulty using and understanding nonverbal behaviors, however, and their pragmatic (social) language skills are typically impaired. As a result, social interactions are quite difficult. Children with Asperger's disorder typically have an overwhelming preoccupation with one or more topics (e.g., dinosaurs, skyscrapers, Egyptology, etc.) and are inflexibly bound by routine. They may have stereotyped mannerisms and/or a persistent preoccupation with parts of objects. This form of ASD also appears more frequently in males (*DSM-IV-TR*, 2000).

Other forms of autism include Rett's Disorder, Childhood Disintegrative Disorder, and Pervasive Developmental Disorder Not Otherwise Specified. According to the *DSM-IV-TR* (2000) Rett's Disorder is a rare neurodegenerative disorder that is believed to be found in females only. It begins with normal development through the first five months of life. This period of normal growth and development is followed by:

> deceleration of head growth between ages 5 and 48 months; loss of previously acquired purposeful hand skills between ages 5 and 30 months with the subsequent development of stereotyped hand movements (e.g., hand-wringing or hand washing); loss of social engagement early in the course (although often social interaction develops later); appearance of poorly coordinated gait or trunk movements; [and] severely impaired expressive and receptive language development with severe psychomotor retardation (p. 77).

Children with Childhood Disintegrative Disorder also appear to start off as healthy babies. After the age of two, however, they begin to regress in multiple areas. By the age of ten, they have had a clinically significant loss of their skills in at least two (but most likely all) of the following areas: social interaction, communication, activities of daily living, bowel or bladder control, play, and/or motor skills (*DSM-IV-TR*). As with autism and Asperger's disorder, this form of ASD is found most often found in boys.

The diagnosis Pervasive Developmental Disorder Not Otherwise Specified (PDD NOS) is given to those children who have some symptoms of an ASD but not enough for a full diagnosis. The diagnosis of PDD NOS, also known as atypical autism, is used when children have unusual symptoms or when their symptoms become apparent at a later age than is typical (*DSM-IV-TR*, 2000). For example, a child who has a severe and pervasive impairment in communication skills or in the development of social interaction skills but who does not meet criteria for specific diagnoses of other ASDs, Schizophrenia, or a personality disorder, such as Schizotypal or Avoidant Personality Disorders could be diagnosed with PDD NOS (*DSM-IV-TR*, 2000). This diagnosis is frequently given to young children who do not clearly meet the diagnosis for Asperger's disorder—like Grace—but who probably will have that diagnosis when they are older.

There are many nuances of ASDs that I have barely touched upon in this brief overview. We will be discussing the primary diagnoses of autism and Asperger's disorder in the following chapters. Fortunately, Rett's Disorder and Childhood Disintegrative Disorder are quite rare, and are outside the scope of this book.

Change Is Coming

As of this writing, the fifth edition of the *DSM* is in development and it proposes to offer significant changes to the way we label children with ASD. The proposed changes include dropping Rett's disorder from the *DSM-V* and putting all other autism diagnoses under one diagnosis: Autistic Disorder or Autism Spectrum Disorder. This proposed changed effectively does away with the diagnoses of Asperger's Disorder and PDD-NOS. The American Psychiatric Association has created a website for the new DSM-V to solicit comments from parents, professionals, and individuals with the disorders (Dsm5.org).

References:

American Psychiatric Association. (2000). *Diagnostic and statistical manual of mental disorders* (4th ed., text rev.). Washington, DC: Author.

American Psychiatric Association. (2010). *DSM-V.* Retrieved from www.dsm5.org/ProposedRevisions/Pages/proposedrevision.aspx?rid=94

Autism Society of America. (2009). *Autism facts.* Retrieved from www.autism-society.org/site/PageServer?pagename=about_home

Cowley, G. (2003, September 8). Girls, boys, and autism. *Newsweek*, 42-50. National Survey on Children's Health (NSCH). (2007). Retrieved from http://nschdata.org/Dataquery/SurveyAreas.aspx?yid=2

CHAPTER THREE

In the Beginning

Realizing That Your Kid Is Different

I knew she cried excessively when both grandmothers wouldn't visit more than 15 minutes and refused to babysit her for even a dinner date. The pediatrician said she might outgrow this phase every three months until she was two. By then it was her "disposition" and nothing more.

— J., CALIFORNIA

Maybe your child is quieter than other children. Then again, maybe he's noisier. Perhaps he rocks back and forth in a way that makes the other children uncomfortable. You notice that she doesn't make eye contact or initiate play with other kids. Maybe a friend has suggested that you have your child assessed. It could be a teacher, or your in-laws, or just your gut. In any event, you know that your child is different. Some things look like delays and other things look like—well, we have no idea what to make of them.

We first pointed out J's differences to our pediatrician ... he told me he was just a fussy baby. Nobody was concerned about him as a young infant but I was terribly concerned since I was with him all the time.

— D., TEXAS

I jokingly called him the "crabbiest little man" I'd ever known when they were doing the evaluation, not knowing that his issues involved so much more than speech. I also noticed that he was not very warm to his family—his hugs were infrequent and he would back into them. He came down ladders backwards. He would sit for hours (if allowed) in front of a TV, totally tuning everything else out. But I didn't think there were really learning issues, as he knew his entire alphabet by the time he was 27 mos. old. Not only did he know the letters, but also he knew the sounds the letters made. I thought then that he would be SOOOO easy to teach!

— A., MINNESOTA

It is hard to put my finger on just how, but he just isn't as mature as other kids his age. Other kids notice it too.

— D., FLORIDA

When he was nine months old, he used to bang his head violently. He never slept thru the night and seemed terrified of baths, and touching or holding him close for comfort seemed to upset him. He was language delayed, although he's got that mastered well now. When he walked, he would stim a lot and meltdowns were a part of his day. Almost anything seemed to set him off.

— J., OHIO

For those of you who don't yet know the Autism Lingo, "stimming" is short for "stimulating," and it generally refers to repetitive behaviors that our kids use to calm themselves. Okay, that's not entirely true. I don't exactly know *why* they do it, but stimming refers to head-banging, rocking, hand-flapping, spinning, and pretty much anything else that is (mostly) harmless but tends to freak out the uninitiated.

One of the reasons that we didn't suspect autism earlier was that Grace didn't rock, flap, or head-bang. She *did* patrol the perimeter of the playground and swing on the swing for an eternity at a time, but by the time we realized that that there was more to this, we were not only in over our heads; we couldn't see dry land in any direction. Admitting this is painful and hard. It's okay to cry buckets, but you won't do that forever. You aren't the only one, believe me. D. in Florida, says:

> *He started exhibiting signs very early, around 3 years old. He was very rigid in his clothing choices, etc. He could not be still, spoke in an overly loud voice most of the time, was delayed in his speech, couldn't get along with siblings, and had no friends of his own. He had many, many meltdowns. I was at my wit's end thinking this was all discipline issues. I cried out to God constantly to show me how to deal with him. After he was diagnosed for ADHD and started taking the meds, he was able to slow down and focus, but many of the other symptoms remained. My biggest challenge was the almost constant meltdowns. It wasn't until after he was diagnosed with Asperger's that I realized that [meltdowns are] part of his disorder and [I] have learned how to deal with them better.*

Paging Dr. Empathy

You are going to become the expert on your child's condition. Actually, guess what? You already are! Fortunately and unfortunately, every kid on the spectrum is a little bit different. Whether you are dealing with a teacher, a doctor, or a neighbor, you do not have to put up with garbage. Do not tolerate anyone who is disrespectful to you, your spouse, or your child. If you don't like them, they aren't going to be able to help you. If you think that they don't know what they're talking about, it doesn't matter if they do; you aren't going to trust them. Go with your gut. Your doctor or therapist isn't going to go home and live with your child 24/7; you are.

Focus on professionals who are willing to train you for that majority of the time when you're on your own. You are your child's first and best advocate, and don't be afraid to stand up for yourself either—or to appreciate the wonderful doctors, therapists, and teachers who can light the path for you. You may feel beaten down and confused, but it's time to go to battle—for your child, for your family, for yourself. Find allies, and don't take any abuse.

> *I would have liked it if any of the therapists we saw had considered for even one moment that his problems might not have been solely attributable to shitty parenting. They would routinely suggest a technique, which I would apply, and which would have no effect at all. After six months of applying a technique with no effect, I would ask for more help, and they'd say, "You just have to stick with it" when I knew it wouldn't keep working. So I'd leave that therapist and look for another one that wasn't a one-trick pony.*
>
> *I wouldn't mind being the source of his issues if only correcting my behavior would have an effect on his. But instead they'd tell me things like "If you give in to his tantrums, he'll keep tantrumming" (which I knew) and then disregard that his three-hour tantrum was over the fact that he had spilled his own milk and that I had offered him more milk. How the heck do you give in to that kind of tantrum? Turn back time? I never would give in, not even once, and yet when I'd point this out, they'd only revert to their own sorry line that they'd memorized back in Shoddy Therapist school.*
>
> — J., MASSACHUSETTS

I wish that I could tell you that the foregoing quote represents an isolated case, but I can't. Many of us (and yes, I do include myself) have encountered professionals who are overly anxious to blame problems on bad parenting. I am so grateful that Dr. DeOrnellas made it clear from the outset that she respected us as the parents. I can't stress this enough. There were times I joked that we came to see her just so someone would tell us that we were doing a good job that week. You, the parent, are the one who has the most opportunity—and, frankly, the obligation—to help your child for the largest amount of time each day, week and month, and time is precious. By the time you are in the office of a professional, you have already seen a lot and been through a lot. If you aren't getting useful insights and practical help within the first few sessions, consider looking elsewhere.

And don't let your in-laws convince you that you're just a terrible parent and that all Junior needs is a good whack in the tush. Give 'em a copy of this book.

If you're a therapist or doctor reading this, of course *you* don't need this gentle reminder, but here it is: *Be Nice.*

I mean it. By the time a family reaches your office, they've been through the wringer. Whether they're super-vigilant parents who are seeing problems that aren't there or whether they're totally asleep at the switch and have been jolted out of their denial by an insistent teacher or a catastrophic event, the fact is: they feel like hell. They have come to you to acknowledge something that no parent wants to admit: namely, that they fear there is something wrong with their child—something that they can't fix. Plus, one of the key features of Asperger's and autism is a lack of empathy, so that's the last thing that they need from you. They're already getting a heaping helping of that from Junior. It took courage for them to even come to you.

While we're on the topic of empathy, let me say as a parent who has been there—heck, I AM there:

This. Is. Not. The. End. Of. The. World.

Honest. You will gain the skills you need with time. In the next chapter, I'll talk about finding the balance between overreacting and under-reacting.

WHAT I WISH I'D KNOWN

IF I COULD GO BACK IN TIME, I WOULD HAVE
TRUSTED MY INSTINCTS MORE WHEN GRACE'S BEHAVIORS
DIDN'T MAKE SENSE. I WOULD HAVE PUSHED HARDER FOR AN
EXPLANATION OF MY CHILD'S DEVELOPMENTAL DELAYS.
THERE'S NO LAW AGAINST VIGILANCE.

As I read back over Bobbi's comments, I am sorry that she and the others have had such bad experiences with professionals. There are only two defenses I can offer for the type of treatment they report. The first is lack of education, training, and/or experience with autism spectrum disorders. The second is a superiority complex on the part of some medical and mental health professionals. I have run into it myself. Psychiatrists, pediatricians, neurologists, psychologists, etc., often don't return my calls either. They're too busy or I'm not important enough—take your choice. When I find one who does and I think he or she is competent, I try hard not to abuse the privilege of calling to chat about clients (patients) we share. I am fortunate to live in a small town with several good professionals—at least some of whom take Medicaid. It's hard to beat that! Unfortunately, their training in autism is limited, and they are having to keep up with the research as it's being printed, just as I am.

This brings us to the first reason. Autism, even though it's been around for a while, is a topic that has only been hot for the past ten to twenty years. When I trained to be a teacher back in the 70s, no one mentioned the word "autism" to me. Students with disabilities were sent to separate schools and we learned very little about them. In the late 80s, when I trained to be a child and family therapist, no one mentioned that I would be seeing children with ASDs. Very few people had heard of Asperger's disorder at that time. A few years later, while earning my

Ph.D. in School Psychology, autism was barely mentioned. It wasn't until I went to work in the schools that I learned about autism. I had a crash course in diagnosing children with autism and providing consultation to parents and teachers. As I learned more and more and spent time with children on the spectrum, I remembered a child I had worked with in college and realized he would have been diagnosed with ASD if we had known what it was. If you do not work with autism, the learning curve is huge—especially for professionals who are trying to keep up to date on fifty million other things.

Just to give you an idea of how much there is to keep up with in this field, from 1981 to 1990 there were just over 2500 articles published on autism in psychology journals. From 1991 to 2000, the number of articles more than doubled. In the past seven years, over 8000 articles on autism research were published. This does not include any of the wonderful books that are being written for parents, teachers, and the general public on the topic of autism.

This is not an excuse for shoddy treatment by professionals. I'm just letting you know how hard it is to stay current with the literature. I certainly don't have time to read it all—nor would I want to. I'm much more interested in spending that time with children and families. I believe that's where the real learning takes place. Nevertheless, as an educator of future school psychologists and a researcher in the field, I do my best to read as much as I can. I just wish there were Cliff's Notes.

There's a saying among those of us who work in the specialty of autism: If you've seen one kid with autism, you've seen one kid with autism. Each of them is different—unique in some wonderful way. If the professional you're working with doesn't see that, try again. There are many of us who just love these kids and their families. We appreciate the struggles you have and we want to help as best we can.

IT BEARS REPEATING

IF YOU'VE SEEN ONE KID WITH AUTISM,
YOU'VE SEEN *ONE KID WITH AUTISM*.

Denial: It Ain't Just a River in Autism

By the time you begin to find meaningful professional help, you have already been dealing with your child's differences for years. How do you balance the importance and benefits of early intervention with the very reasonable possibility that your child is going to outgrow her little quirks? How do you find the balance between hysteria and denial? How do you reconcile your desire to help your child with the knowledge that, if perfect families actually exist, they aren't people you'd want to hang out with anyway?

Nobody Wakes Up with Their Hair Already Done

I'm going to let you in on one of the secrets that nobody told me. This one goes right up there with how painful childbirth *really is* and the fact that everybody has fights on their honeymoon. Want to know another secret? I'll whisper: everybody's kids have "something wrong" with them. One of my friends had to explain this one to me. I was a little slow on the uptake. I even tested her:

"What about so-and-so? They're perfect. There ain't nothing wrong with them."

"Oh, Bobbi, come on. *They're not nice.*"

Yes, we are sometimes overwhelmed. Okay, it is probably more accurate to say that the word "overwhelmed" was invented to describe parenting a child with autism. On the other hand, everybody's got something. I, for one, wouldn't trade.

There is no reason to be afraid of our known struggles because we're looking right at them. When you are tempted to feel envious of people who have neurologically typical kids (that's "NT" in Autism Lingo and it refers to so-called "normal" kids), take a deep breath and think of all of the ways that things can and do go wrong with supposedly perfect kids. I'm not trying to be ugly or begrudge them; I'm just trying to tell you that nobody gets out of parenting unscathed. Nobody's life is really like the LookatWhataPerfectMomIAm.com blogs. When I was a child, I watched the Brady Bunch and wished that I could wake up in the morning with perfect hair. It took me waaaay too many years to learn that nobody actually does.

The First Step Can Be the Hardest

Sometimes, it's impossible to see something that's right in front of your face. There is no point in beating yourself up over this. It happens to the best of us. If it's normal to be clueless, I am *extra* normal.

> *I had known a few children with severe autism. I was a substitute teacher one year and taught in my daughter's kindergarten class. There was a severely autistic child in the class and it was so hard to concentrate in there when he engaged in some of his "strange" behaviors. He got angry at my daughter once for an unknown reason and he sort of mimed punching her over and over until someone could stop him. Luckily, he never actually made contact with her, but the experience frightened both of us. I thought that having him in the classroom was scary and overwhelming for students and teacher alike (although the teacher did an incredible job with him!). If you had suggested to me that my perfect son, who was in 3rd grade at the time, had autism, I would have said you were out of your mind!*
>
> — L., TEXAS

Speaking for myself, understanding came in stages. First, I had to see that my child needed help that I wasn't yet equipped to give. From that point, it was obvious that I needed to do whatever it took to get equipped. This is very painful for a parent. Mommy and Daddy are supposed to at least know what's going on. It's hard to observe, and it's hard to hear from someone else. Some of us respond like A. in Texas:

Principal at school pointed [it] out. I did not like it one bit. I dismissed the idea that he was socially not appropriate in his behaviors.

As for me, my irritation quickly gave way to terror. As I began to get a handle on all that I didn't know, I felt fear. Real fear. That's when it's very helpful to have a reality check. "What if my child is twelve and dropping rocks off an overpass onto cars? What if she really doesn't understand that it would be wrong to do that?" I tearfully asked my friend Sara. She, being the mom of seven, wryly pointed out that my worries wouldn't really be that different from the worries of ANY mom of a twelve-year-old, now, would they?

The lessons continued, but they didn't get easier. After applying myself as diligently as I could, I gradually came to the sobering realization (prepare for another Duh! moment) that I could read every book, talk to every doctor, and create every therapeutic tool in the world and it wasn't going to change the fundamental structure of my baby's brain. I may be Mommy, but there is no "all better" here. It doesn't work that way. Whether you want to use the word "normal," or "neurotypical" (NT for short), my kid ain't that. We shouldn't be surprised when we have a strong emotional response to the challenges of parenting an autistic child.

I am desperately trying to learn his language, and to teach him mine, but I am not a saint and sometimes I lose my temper.
— R., NOTTINGHAM, UK

Accepting that was sad and freeing at the same time. Having a child with autism is a challenge, not a tragedy. Once I gave myself the freedom to mourn the picture of the family that I thought I was going to have—an illusion I never realized I'd harbored in the first place—it became much easier to get on with the realities of my new life. While it might have seemed catastrophic, grim, or even impossible at first, it's actually none of those things. As the parent, I am not in a position to fix, to cure, to change my kid. None of those things are possible, nor are they necessary. Rather, I have to learn to drum to the beat of a different marcher. My child isn't broken; she's just her own unique, irreplaceable self. As one of the moms wrote in *Home Educating Our Autistic Spectrum Children: Paths Are Made by Walking,* most of the problem seems to evaporate when I stop expecting her to act normally. Yes, we work for our kids to recover from some of the symptoms of autism, but I don't talk about cures. As I write this chapter, a larger segment of the world is discovering Dr. Temple Grandin, and this is a good thing. She has said that the world needs all kinds of minds, including autistic ones. The longer I live with my Grace, the more I agree with Dr. Grandin. While there are many ways to work with your child's challenges—and we introduce you to a lot of them in this book—he is who he is, and that's not a bad thing. Honest.

The Awful Truth

Gentle reader, it's early in our relationship, so let me just warn you: when I hit a nerve, I cut straight through to the bone. I'm going to do that now. One of the reasons it's so hard to be the parent of a child who is both different and exhausting is what it says about *you.* You aren't going to be the light-hearted, almost unMom-like cool mom who is mistaken as the sister of her prom-queen/valedictorian daughter who is verbal, compliant, precocious, athletic, and basically a star in multiple socially rewarding areas. You aren't going to be the dad of the impeccably behaved quarterback-scholar who puts military-school grads to shame. No, at least for the time being, you are the load-bearing, Quit-Staring-At-My-Kid parent. It hurts. I know. This is as good a time as any to introduce you to the Autism Prayers authored by Elizabeth Burton Scott, author of a couple of wonderful books on autism. When it all gets too intense, check out: www.rdrpublishers.com/autism_prayers.html.

WHAT I WISH I'D KNOW

GOING FROM "THERE'S NOTHING WRONG HERE"
TO "THE SKY IS FALLING!" IS JARRING. FREAKING OUT A BIT
IS NORMAL. IT WON'T ALWAYS BE A SHOCK TO YOUR SYSTEM.
YOU CAN'T MEASURE YOUR ENTIRE FUTURE—OR YOUR CHILD'S—
BY THE WAY THAT YOU FEEL AT THIS MOMENT. ONCE YOU START
TO KNOW WHERE ALL OF THIS IS HEADED, IT DOES GET EASIER.

Early Intervention Is Critical

As you would with any other medical, educational or psychological need, you will want to deal with folks who know what they're talking about. This is easier said than done, but we found someone who had treated patients for years, was associated with a school for kids on the autism spectrum, and had published in the area. Also, she let us know right off the bat that she didn't think that our family was deranged, and that she didn't intend to make a career out of us.

Nobody Puts Grace in a Corner

Personal recommendations are worth their weight in gold—although once you arrive at that office, the only references that really count are those of you and your child. Don't stick with anyone who doesn't like or respect your child—or you. While some folks need more face time in the office than others, we were impressed that Dr. DeOrnellas didn't plan to make a career out of us. She has never, ever encouraged us to become dependent upon her. To the contrary, we understood from the beginning that parent training was going to be as much of a focus as any of her dealings with our child. Unless you can afford to bring your health care provider home with you, you are going to need to be trained and built up for that vast majority of time when he or she is not around. You may feel clueless, but you are already much more of an expert on your child than anyone else is, and you will be educating your pediatrician, your child's teachers, and your in-laws as you go. You may be shocked at the response of seemingly intelligent adults, especially professionals and in-laws.

> *We saw five therapists, two psychopharmacologists, several teachers, one psychologist, and one pediatrician. No one wanted to go out on a limb and diagnose him. Some people wanted to medicate, "and if that helps, we'll assume he has something the medication treats." The only thing fruitful was whatever I read for myself when I did research. I rabbit-trailed through the internet looking for ANYTHING that might explain his behavior patterns. I was told consistently that he could "not" have Asperger's even though he had all but two of the symptoms.*
>
> — J., Massachusetts

Let's say you've found the perfect psychologist for your family. For the sake of this discussion, we'll call her "Dr. D." Now it is time to talk with the insurance company. Perhaps you talked to them first, but it's so nice, you'll have to do it twice—at least. Don't stop at the first "no" when dealing with your insurance company. It isn't unusual for parents to pay $10,000.00 per year or more for treatment, and most people can't afford this. As with everything else, you have to be an advocate for your child—and for yourself. Do not feel helpless if what you're hearing doesn't ring true—whether it's from a doctor, an insurance company, or anyone else. You may need a second—and sometimes an eighth—opinion.

I was impressed, shocked, and sometimes moved to tears by the stories told by parents in *Home Educating Our Autistic Spectrum Children: Paths Are Made By Walking.* This book, which is a collection of essays edited by Terri Dowty and Kitt Cowlishaw (Jessica Kingsley Publishers 2002), is the unvarnished truth about parents, kids, and their interactions with teachers, doctors, and psychologists. Even if you've never considered home schooling, I would recommend this book; I found it to be a welcome "reality check" about what I might expect from thirteen families who have been farther down this road than I have.

In Defense of Teachers

Some parents begin investigating at the urging of a kindergarten or first-grade teacher. While it may be painful for you to hear that Mrs. Pickle thinks that Herman is too much of a disruption or Emily is in her own little world, and you may think that the teacher is just plain wrong, there is no harm in giving Mrs. Pickle a fair hearing. Let me say this up front: I am a great fan of teachers. I come from a long line of teachers. As a home schooling parent, I am not just a fan of teachers; I'm a teacher myself.

If you have entrusted your child to another adult for most of his waking hours during the week, it seems reasonable to me that you should respect that adult's observations and opinions. Call me crazy, but that preschool teacher not only observes your three-year-old all day long; she also observes *other* three-year-olds all day long, and she may have a better idea of what's "normal" than a doting and/or anxious parent would. Then again, if you find that what you're hearing from this person just doesn't ring true, your child may need another teacher to be with all day long. But before you assume that this is the case, you should at least hear the teacher out.

Once you've heard her out, you may disagree, but it is probably worthwhile to follow up on her observations and recommendations. After all, she may be more objective than Mommy and Daddy (ouch!), and she has seen lots of other kids and how they function. If she's quick to condemn your child for merely being shy or quirky, that's not the teacher you want for your child in the first place. If you respect her enough to place your child under her supervision and care, you should at least give consideration to her point of view before rejecting it out of hand. Okay, I've beaten you up enough about this; you get the idea.

On the Other Hand

Having now defended teachers, which I will generally do, I must also share an insight that I read in *Home Educating Our Autistic Spectrum Children: Paths Are Made by Walking,* which is unfortunately consistent with the moms I know. Here goes: parents complain that they spend most of their time trying to educate their kids' teachers about autism spectrum disorders, while the teachers are spending most of their time trying to convince Junior to "act normal." Ouch. If this shoe fits, maybe there's another way to think about Junior's behavior and what is really important to address.

All I can say is that Bobbi is right. You are the expert on your child. I know more than you do about autism and I know lots of kids with autism, but you know more than I will ever know about *your child*. Nothing you tell a professional about your child should be dismissed. That doesn't mean a professional will agree with you all the time. Sometimes, I can point out something to a parent that they are too close to see. When you're living the experience it's hard to understand the big picture. A good professional can help you do that. So can other parents who've walked the path ahead of you.

If you haven't established a support system, do that now. You're going to need it. Maybe not right this minute, but somewhere down the line—like tomorrow. Other parents are hungry to share their experiences with you and are happy to help share your load. Good professionals should be a part of your support system and you can learn who they are by talking to other parents. Nothing your child is doing is going to be any weirder than something their child has already done. Don't be afraid to reach out to other people.

IT BEARS REPEATING

DON'T BE AFRAID TO REACH OUT TO OTHER PARENTS.
NOTHING YOUR CHILD IS DOING IS GOING TO BE
ANY WEIRDER THAN SOMETHING THEIR OWN CHILD
HAS ALREADY DONE. REALLY.

CHAPTER FOUR

The Causes of Autism

Paging Dr. Freud

Beginning, of course, with the premise that *everything* is Mommy's fault, in this chapter we will discuss questions like "why is there such an explosion in the diagnosis of autism spectrum disorders all of a sudden?" There are many theories: vaccinations, pesticides, past under-diagnosis, present over-diagnosis, genetics, diet, advanced paternal age, advanced maternal age, etc.—but we encourage you, gentle reader, to reach your own conclusions (with lots of guidance from Dr. DeOrnellas).

The Only Theory of Causation That Everyone Agrees Upon Is … I Can't Think of Anything

Jan Fortune-Wood, in *Home Educating Our Autistic Spectrum Children,* makes at least a partial explanation for the recent explosion in the diagnosis of ASDs that is, I think, brilliant in its simplicity; she posits that what used to be called "bullies" are now labeled ADHD and what used to be called "nerds" or victims of the bullies are now called "Asperger's" (p. 219). While there is certainly more to it than that, it's an interesting starting point.

Way back in the 1980s, when I was in college, the only mention of autism I heard was a passing reference to it as a rare subcategory of childhood schizophrenia. There was one book about autism, in which *leading authority* Bruno Bettelheim taught us that autism was caused by refrigerator mothers, and that the poor souls afflicted with autism were "locked fortresses." I remember someone raising his hand in Abnormal Psych and asking the professor, "But what happens to those kids when they grow up? I've never heard of an autistic adult." The professor frowned as if it had never occurred to him that an autistic child would actually grow up, and then said slowly, "I guess you'd just call them schizophrenic. That's kind of a garbage-can diagnosis when they don't know what to say. They'd be institutionalized long-term, of course." It's hard for me to even fathom how the conventional wisdom could have been so backwards, so wrong, such a short time ago.

I said I wasn't gonna take a position, but Bruno Bettelheim was wrong ("locked fortress") and Temple Grandin is right. I will have lots more to say about Dr. Grandin, but for now, I will tell you that she is brave, sensitive, brilliant, accomplished, and that she has done more than any other person to educate the world about autism. Oh, and did I mention that she is autistic? She was, for me, the first-person voice of autism before my child found her own voice.

Let's move on to seeking help.

When you get a bunch of parents talking, you will hear a lot of opinions about what works and what doesn't work. Everyone seems to agree that early intervention is critical. What kind of intervention? How do you know what will help your child?

Don't limit yourself by the ideas that you had before you had kids, or even what seems sensible based on your prior parenting experiences. Most of what I knew from prior parenting experience actually worked against me when it came to Grace, and gems can be found in funny places. My daughter gets a lot of benefit from lying on her tummy on a spinning disc and wearing a full-body sock apparatus, both of which look quite nutty to the casual observer (or to pretty much anyone, including us). Sometimes, she delights in using both of them at the same time.

Other insights may come from professionals or other parents, or both. A couple of years back, I went to a conference and there were three different sessions focused on autism spectrum disorders and ADHD. At one of the sessions, the speaker was a fascinating lady named Jan Bedell. She asked the parents to raise their hands if their kids had never crawled. More than half of the parents in the room—including me—raised our hands. Her theory, which I will try not to butcher by relating it in my own words, was that many neurological disorders are caused by (or look like) the two hemispheres of the brain not working together in concert, and that crawling is actually a very sophisticated movement that requires cooperation between the two halves of the brain. She recommended that we take "crawling breaks" with our kids to retrain their brains. I think that this really helped my kid. I do. That sounds as least as sane as anything else I've heard, especially in light of the fact that it took Grace six years (and an infant brother to race with) to learn how to crawl. For years, when I could get her to try, her attempts looked more like a downward-facing dog pose in motion. It made me think that Ms. Bedell might just be on to something.

There are a million theories about what causes autism. I could relate some of them to my own family, although I suspect that it has the most to do with genetics—the parents that Grace picked. Here goes:

- Hair dye? Check (not in the first trimester, but check).
- Plastic cups? Check.
- Old mom? Check.
- Living near power lines? I don't know. How close do you have to be?
- Old dad (who happens to be an engineer)? Check.

- Vaccinations? Half-check.

- Tough pregnancy? OH yeah.

- Diet? Check, then uncheck, then check again.

- Disposable diapers? Check, for five years.

- Too many sonograms? Not only check, but this one could have me in the corner with my thumb in my mouth if I thought about it long enough. Remember back in Chapter One, when I told you that my pregnancy with Grace was medically difficult? Eeek.

- And, my personal nightmare, the one time I sprayed a hornet's nest before I knew I was pregnant? Yes, check. If I think about that one too long, I'll wake up screaming at 2 a.m.

Let me be on the record as saying that *I have no answers*. The person who does should win some large, lucrative prizes. On the other hand, the current explosion of autism spectrum disorders is so large—it can't be attributed solely to improved diagnostic awareness.

I've heard all of these conjectures about the cause of ASDs—with the exception of the disposable diapers—and I think most trace back to our unquenchable desire to know WHY? Why is our child different? If we can blame it on something, we don't have to take a hard look at ourselves and we can relax a little.

That said, I'm going to try to fill in as many blanks as possible with what we know for sure.

First, are we diagnosing more children with autism than ever before? Yes.

Why? Because we know more and we're better at it than we used to be. Also, we're widening the net. We're no longer looking only at autism. We're including all of the ASDs. This is a good thing—it means more children and families are going to get help. I'm going out on a limb here and say that I believe we are still missing some children and that the rate of children being diagnosed may go even higher. One of my next forays into research is to look at girls with HFASD (high-functioning autism spectrum disorders). I think we're missing a lot of them. It is only in the past year or so that we are starting to see books come out about girls with Asperger's disorder. In my experience, their profiles just look different than the boys' do, and they're being missed.

I also believe we are missing a lot of adults with Asperger's disorder. Since the non-German-speaking population didn't know about Asperger's disorder until the 1980s, there are a lot of adults who could have been diagnosed but weren't. I have seen a number of them who began to make the connection (or had a spouse who pointed it out to them) when their child was diagnosed. But I digress. ...

Are we over-diagnosing autism? Maybe, in some cases.

However, I don't run into too many children that have been misdiagnosed. It may be different where you live, but around here I think we're doing a pretty good job. One exception: I occasionally have seen parents seek a diagnosis of autism for their child who is mentally retarded. Their reasons vary. For some, I think it is easier to say they have a child with autism than a child who is mentally retarded. Also, in some areas there are better services for children with ASD.

Do vaccines cause autism? No.

As unpopular as it may be to say this, there is currently no evidence to say they do and lots of evidence to say they don't. A recent ruling by the U.S. Court of Claims stated that vaccines do not cause autism and this ruling was based on years of scientific study.

Do hair dyes, plastic cups, electric towers, disposable diapers, etc., cause autism? No.

I don't know of any research that says they do and I would say they do not. Why? Because autism is so widespread. As Ritvo says, "We have found autism and Asperger's disorders in every corner of the world where we have looked. And they affect all races, and have no special respect or preference for social class, religion, or income level" (2006, p. 26).

WHAT WE CAN BE PRETTY SURE ABOUT

It bears repeating here that ASDs are neurological disorders and that is where many of the research dollars are being spent. Although it is outside the focus of this book, there are many, many research studies being conducted on the brains of individuals with ASDs right now. This is not an area of expertise (or even particular interest) for me, but it is cutting edge and we will be reading the results in the next few years. This particular area of study first began in the 1960s when it was noticed that many children with autism also have epilepsy. It is now understood that there is a clear relationship between autism and epilepsy and that up to one-third of individuals with ASDs have a seizure disorder (Tuchman, Moshe, & Rapin, 2009). Other research has looked at brain size, sensory modulation, motor functioning, attention, and executive function. An example of the more recent findings is that "increased brain size may be related to anomalies in cortical connectivity" (Hardan, Muddasani, Vemulapalli, Keshavan, & Minshew, cited in Kestenbaum, 2008, p. 284).

Genetics play a big role in ASDs, and we're going to be even more sure about this in a few years. We still don't know which genes are involved, but that is just a matter of time. As evidence, in identical or monozygotic twins, the heritability concordance is 60% to 90%, while in dyzygotic twins, the rate is less than 5% (Kestenbaum).

A number of studies are being conducted to evaluate the role genetics plays in the cause of ASDs. Gillberg (1991) has studied families of children with ASDs going back several generations. He found that varying degrees of ASDs can show up in the same family. For example, one family member can have severe autism while another has Asperger's disorder.

So you're right—he is just like his father!

I am willing to admit what I don't know. Heck, I've been exposing areas of my past and current ignorance to you, gentle reader, for many tens of pages now. I simply don't have enough of the science under my belt to form an intelligent opinion on the topic (and believe me, I'm considering a lot of different theories and arguments). I see no harm in taking a good, hard look at any medical treatments or recommendations relating to any of my kids. While I've looked pretty long and hard at many approaches, this is an area where one person's experience may be literally useless to the next person.

In my personal case, Grace's autism is not the regressive type that I most often hear about in connection with allegations about vaccines or other environmental factors. While I'm opinionated, I am genuinely on the fence on this one, although Dr. DeOrnellas' opinion carries a great deal of weight with me, especially when it comes to what will and won't work with Grace.

We have explored dietary modifications, and have taken multiple runs at the GFCF (that's gluten-free, casein-free) diet and its first cousin, the DAN! Diet. Yep, no wheat and no dairy. Too many people have been helped by these regimens for me to ignore them. While these regimens are daunting at first, some people swear by them, telling me that they help with everything from verbal symptoms to bowel control. Unfortunately for us, so far, our only measurable result was a little girl who was very crabby about not being able to eat some of the few foods she's actually willing to eat in the first place. Anyway, we are now back to our regular diet, armed with garlic salt (yuck, I know, but she even asks for it on weird things like Cheerios, and a ritual shake has been known to help the dinner go down).

What moved me to engage in some very expensive testing and to try the diet again (okay, to try it in a more intelligent and systematic way and to give it a fair chance) is the idea that, since my Grace is challenged in the area of appreciating pain and other physical sensations, she might have some bad stomachaches that she can't even really distinguish from feeling generally crummy. In any event, if it had worked for us, we'd be shouting from the rooftop about it. The fact that it didn't impact my kid doesn't mean that you shouldn't try it. I have heard the most success stories about these diets from parents whose kids who were quite nonverbal and/or had regressive autism. While neither of those things are the case with my child, the diet certainly didn't harm her.

The interest in the GFCF diet is based on a finding that there is a subset of individuals with ASDs who also have celiac disease. Celiac disease is an immune-mediated, chronic, multisystemic disorder triggered by gluten ingestion in genetically predisposed individuals (Barcia, Posar, Santucci, & Parmeggiani, 2008, p. 407). The prevalence rate for celiac disease ranges from 1 in 150 to 1 in 250 individuals in the United States (Barcia et al.). Research has indicated cases of autism with celiac disease and cases of autism without celiac disease.

Barcia and colleagues randomly tested 150 individuals with an ASD for celiac disease and found that five of them tested positive. Only three of the five were having gastrointestinal symptoms at the time. Although five doesn't sound like very many, the rate is much higher than for the general population. Once diagnosed, the five individuals with ASD and celiac disease maintained a gluten-free diet for at least six months. The three individuals who had gastrointestinal symptoms saw an improvement; however, none of the five had any improvement in their behavioral symptoms (Barcia et al.). My recommendation (and that of Barcia et al.) is to talk to your child's pediatrician about having him evaluated for celiac disease if you think it may be a problem or if you have family members with the disease.

Bottom line: Grace and I can't be your guinea pigs on this one, folks. If you are so inclined, you'll just have to try it and/or research it yourselves. As I'll discuss in more detail elsewhere, I avoid things that might hurt my kid and I'm pretty open about trying things that might help. One thing I've learned to avoid is the *"You're a bad parent if you don't do what worked for my kid"* kind of parent. There are more than a few of them out there, I'm sorry to report.

Many parents of children with ASD have explored what are known as complementary and alternative medicine (CAM) treatments. They tend to be controversial and most have not been proven effective by rigorous research methods. CAM treatments include secretin, gluten-free/casein-free diets, chelation, special vitamins, auditory integration therapy, music therapy, hyperbaric oxygen, magnetic therapy, and others.

Christon, Mackintosh, and Myers (2010) surveyed 248 parents of children with ASD to see if they had used CAM treatments and how they viewed the results. The researchers found that over 70% had tried at least one type of CAM treatment and over half were using a CAM treatment at the time. Each parent who had tried a CAM treatment reported they had started the treatment with high expectations even though many had only anecdotal information from other parents as to whether it would be effective. Some parents felt that their children did get better with CAM treatment but the reason most parents stopped the treatment was that it did not work for their child (Christon et al.). While it is possible that some children were helped, others may have had no effect or have even been harmed by the treatments. More research is needed to determine the effectiveness of CAM treatments and parents are encouraged to be careful in implementing controversial, unproven treatments.

Fun and Folly with Self-Diagnosis

Either there's some heredity at work here or Grace definitely picked the right family. My adorable, beloved husband is, in his own words, "a little bit Aspergy." This might explain how, in his forties, he was sufficiently self-contained to successfully complete a very challenging graduate program while having me and two toddlers as roommates. Ben has been known to stick with one topic long after everyone's eyes have glazed over, and he has an ability to focus that has served him very, very well in his professional life. He cannot bear for me to throw anything away, and he is not comfortable with change in general. He has very, very definite ideas about things that make no difference to me; for example, he picked out every single stem of our wedding flowers, and it took the first five years of our marriage for him to select a kitchen table. (He had opinions about it; I didn't, so we bumbled along with the bachelor table until it became so gross that I developed an opinion—an insistent one.) He's also a genius. In other words, Aspergy. Very, very Aspergy.

BEN SAYS

I WAS VERY HAPPY WITH OUR EXPERIENCED TABLE.
IT ALSO HIT MY PRICE POINT.

Ben was slow to see that there was anything unusual to Grace's behavior because it all seemed so familiar to him. For example, I told him I had learned that it's not a good idea to take Grace to the movie theater. Before I could even describe how overwhelmed her ears and other senses were, he was nodding vigorously, saying, "Oh, yeah, that's painful."

BEN SAYS

FOR THE LONGEST TIME, GRACE AND I WERE GETTING ALONG
SO WELL THAT I DIDN'T REALIZE THAT SHE WASN'T TALKING.

My husband is very sensitive to bodily sensations. Sometimes I think he's got K's situation with the exception that he's highly congenial publicly. He's highly positive at home too so he's a very socially acceptable person. However, he must be shrill about the "feel of the sheets" and other things that seem a non-issue to me. I had to buy a series of high-thread-count-Egyptian-cotton sheets until he felt one was just right. There are many examples of my husband being this way about rugs, clothes, etc.

— J., California

Take Those Stinkin' Things Off

But the thing that really convinced me—that would be the headphones. Let me explain. They were more like earmuffs. They were the kind of headphones that one wears at a gun range. They were the kind of headphones that made him able to pretend that none of the rest of us was in our 800-square-foot campus apartment. I took those headphones as a personal affront—nay, a rejection. When he graduated and we moved to a spacious house with more than two hundred square feet per family member, the headphones came with him. He wanted to wear them in his home office, and sometimes—Egads!—even into the common areas of the house. They had become his comfort object. I gave him an ultimatum. (He does still wear them at work, or at least he did until he read this.) As the next couple of years unfolded and I began to understand more about our daughter, I also gained some empathy for Ben. Don't get the wrong idea; they're still not allowed back in the house. I'm just sayin' I understand.

BEN SAYS

I AM EXTREMELY DISTRACTED BY CONVERSATIONS,
AND THE HEADPHONES ARE VERY EFFECTIVE
AT SUPPRESSING VOICES, ESPECIALLY THOSE
OF MY ADORABLE WIFE AND CHILDREN.

Your Child Has an Autism Spectrum Disorder, and Chances Are, So Do You!

What about me? I was surprised to realize that I have several Aspergian traits myself. (As you may already be saying, duh.) I'm a verbal (okay, verbose), social, empathic English major who went to law school to avoid math. No Asperger's here. Uh, look again. When you look below my surface, I do have a strong affinity for my own company, I make rapid and interesting (okay, strange) associations, I lack fashion sense, and I crave familiarity. I have a sense of smell like a dog, and my hearing is very acute; these senses seem to have borrowed from my eyes, my taste, and my tactile sense. I can be cluelessly compulsive; let's just say that if there were an extended siege of my house, we are in no danger of running out of such items as oatmeal, books, or children's clothing. I am sure that I could have been described as socially immature as a child; I played with dolls long past the age when other girls had moved on to clothes, makeup, and boys, and I still don't really get the clothes and makeup part. (Boys are now quite okay, especially the one I'm married to.) When I was a teenager, I developed a "nervous tic" in response to stress that was alarming to a close friend and her mother. While I was both embarrassed and bothered by my behavior, it was uncontrollable for months, and then I was able to control it only with great effort. Yes, I have stimmed.

While I would describe myself as social, I am and I ain't. My passions—reading, writing, and exercise—are things that I pursue in a very solitary fashion, as were my youthful preoccupations with television and food. Anyone who knows me can tell you of my ability to latch onto a topic and shake it to death with the ferocity of a deranged canine, yea, even to the point of writing a book about it.

We moved a lot when I was a child, and I (unintentionally) picked up every accent from every place we lived while making almost no friends. I have an uncanny memory for worthless minutiae, which takes up a disproportionate amount of space in my brain where a sense of direction should be. I am at least as comfortable with animals as I am with people.

Probably most convincingly, *I married my husband*. There are now several books in print about Asperger's marriages. One of the theories that made me smile was the idea that people on the spectrum often marry outside their culture, which happens to be the case with my marriage. The theory holds that they attribute the communication differences that they encounter in courtship to language or cultural differences instead of realizing that one or both members of the couple are neurologically different. In *Thinking in Pictures,* Temple Grandin—who is, in my humble opinion, never wrong about such things—makes the case for persons on the autism spectrum marrying one another, remaining single, or choosing to marry someone who is eccentric. Whether I veer closer to the "eccentric" or the "fellow Aspergian" category, all that I can tell you is that it works. I'm leaning toward "eccentric," but some days it's a toss-up. Hey, I'm a writer. I think that pretty much establishes the whole eccentric-solitary thing. Unable to decide, I took a totally non-scientific approach and did a couple of online questionnaires. Then I prevailed upon my dear husband to answer a few questions. Apparently, we are both overachievers, and I'm autistic-er than he is!

I'm going to let you in on a secret. (Heck, by this point, you know most of my secrets anyway.) All of that embarrassing trivia about me in the preceding paragraphs—it's actually one of the most powerful tools that I have in accepting and relating to my kid. Here, I must recommend to you the "Mark's Mum" story from *Paths Are Made by Walking*. As she tells the story of her son's reality in her matter-of-fact voice, she gradually lets you know that she shares his unusual experience of the world. It is as touching, poignant, and real as it gets. As she's describing autism, you gradually realize that she is talking about "We" and not "You." When she got to the part about finding her "normal" sister totally illogical and weird, I had to wipe away tears as I giggled at her description. I have shamelessly stolen one of her ideas by talking to my children about how I can be a little autistic too sometimes. To the extent that the label may be stigmatizing rather than enlightening, I think that it helps all of us to know that we're in this together, there's nothing wrong with us, and it doesn't have to define our lives. For me, being able to say to my child, "Yeah, I'm sort of autistic too," has helped me to feel closer to her. You may also be surprised to find how many other people will reach out to you if you are open about having autism in the family. There are a lot of us out there, and we need each other.

Whether I am an Aspie myself or merely a carrier, this is all pretty familiar to me. Both sides of our family tree are full of odd, solitary, brilliant types who seem totally normal to us. (To all of my relatives and in-laws who may be reading this, *of course* I'm not referring to *you,* except for the brilliant part, naturally.). My dad, who has most of the Bible committed to memory, is not an adventurous eater and has been known to have a favorite topic or two, and to be solitary in nature, disappeared for four hours at Grace's baptism party. All of the other guests were gone when he happily strolled up and was ready to take my mom home. The amazing thing is that none of us objected or even thought it was unusual. In a recent conversation with my mom, I was telling her that my research shows that many kids with ASD have problems with handwriting, particularly cursive (for those of you across the pond, that's "joined writing"). I told her that I planned to teach Grace to type at a young age. She told me that, from the earliest grades, teachers threatened to refuse to grade my work because it was completely illegible. (More on Grace's surprising handwriting journey later.)

Uh, yeah. It's my *husband* who's the Aspie.

Right.

REFERENCES

Barcia, G., Posar, A., Santucci, M., & Parmeggiani, A. (2008). *Autism and celiac disease. Journal of Autism and Developmental Disorders, 38,* 407-408.

Christon, L. M., Mackintosh, V. H., & Myers, B. J. (2010). Use of complementary and alternative medicine (CAM) treatments by parents of children with autism spectrum disorders. *Research in Autism Spectrum Disorders, 4,* 249-259.

Gillberg, C. (1991). Clinical and neurobiological aspects of Asperger's syndrome in six family studies. In U. Frith (Ed.). *Autism and Asperger's syndrome* (pp. 122-146). Cambridge, UK: Cambridge University Press.

Kestenbaum, C. J. (2008). Autism, Asperger's, and other oddities…thoughts about treatment approaches. *Journal of the American Academy of Psychoanalysis and Dynamic Psychiatry, 36*(2), 279 294.

Ritvo, E. (2006). *Understanding the nature of autism and Asperger's disorder.* London, UK: Jessica Kingsley Publishers.

Tuchman, R., Moshe, S. L., & Rapin, I. (2009). Convulsing toward the pathophysiology of autism. *Brain and Development, 31,* 95-103.

CHAPTER FIVE

The Basics ...
with a Twist of Autism

No Thanks; I'll Just Have a Banana.
With Garlic Salt.

It is common for our kids to have marked food preferences. This is yet another area in which I have learned not to judge my fellow parents. I know kids who have a list of acceptable foods that doesn't use up all of their counting fingers. My child has a strong preference for smooth, bland/sweet and room temperature foods. When I say "strong preference," I intend for you to call up a mental picture of hunger strikes accompanied by lots of screaming.

Baby-Steppin'

We work with one food and one attribute at a time. Sometimes it takes months or even years to introduce a new food, or even a new texture. For example, since she liked bananas, we introduced "crispy bananas" (sugarless banana chips). We count this as two foods, and she has been known to eat them together and consider it to be a meal. Then we moved on to trying to introduce other crunchy foods or to put something else with them. Since she is fond of French fries, we have learned to roast other vegetables (this is very, very easy—toss 'em in a little oil and bake 'em at 400 degrees for about twenty minutes and serve with salt). She now asks for—get this!—roasted Brussels sprouts. This is a perfect example of how parenting a kid on the autism spectrum is like parenting any other child, *only more so*: you have to break things down into the tiniest pieces, and then break them down even further, to present them to your child. Borrowing a line from Mark Twain, make things as simple as possible, but no simpler. On second thought, go ahead and make them simpler.

We also associate new things with positive things and take tiny, tiny steps. For example, when Grace was younger, I would wrap her in her Special Blanket and hold her while I introduced one new food. We successfully added golden raisins to her repertoire this way. (Oh, yes, they are very, very different from black raisins.) They went into her oatmeal ("porridge") right along with the dates and raisins that she already liked. Another example is chicken nuggets, which are (regrettably) a favorite among most little kids. These were the first meat that she was willing to eat. Since we're not major meat eaters anyway, it seemed logical for us to mix in some soy "chicken" nuggets, and she now eats them too.

We relish the small victories. When we would hit a fast food joint, she kept ordering a "cheeseburger" and then not touching it. Through trial and error, we learned that what she wanted was a cheese sandwich, with ONLY bread and cheese. There is, incidentally, only one color and shape of cheese that is acceptable. Grace recently had a memorable meltdown in the dairy section of the grocery store because her sister picked up a bag of cheese that was both the wrong shape and the wrong color. Just seeing it in the hands of a family member was appalling to her.

Guess the Fruit

If you're looking to branch out, I recommend that you start with fruit. We have been able to leverage her love of sweetness to introduce her to many, many fruits. Sometimes, especially if her siblings are cooperating, we play Guess the Fruit. *Open your mouth and close your eyes, and you will get a big surprise!* Note that all options must be acceptable to your youngster's palate, unless you're in the mood to wear them. This also does not work when she's in a bad mood, or when she hasn't had a chance to eyeball the range of options on her plate to confirm that everything there is something she's willing to eat. As with many other things, she seems more receptive at certain times of day (in our case, the morning).

DJ Mom Presents: The Remix

When we eat cheese sandwiches at home, we might substitute whole-grain or sprouted bread, use soy cheese, or put them on her favorite plate. Sometimes this is met with pleasure, and other times it is not. Once we got her to start eating Lion Sandwiches (raisins and shredded cheese on top of a bread item of some sort), we began to mix in some shredded carrots ("for more realistic color in the lion's mane," we assured her), and she ate some of them too. You'd also be surprised at where you can slip a teaspoon of pureed yams (a grilled cheese or peanut butter sandwich, for starters). To get her to try something new, I have also been shameless about where I will add garlic salt.

In Praise of Vitamins

We are also huge fans of whole food supplementation (see your local natural food store for dozens of options), especially since my daughter is willing to eat them. As with the general improvements to our diet, this is an example of how having an ASD in the family has actually improved the way that we take care of ourselves and our entire family.

Quality Time at the Piggly Wiggly

For a while, I made Grace my grocery store buddy. It worked for a time, before her sensory issues made the sights and acoustics of the grocery store unbearable to her—which, in turn, made the experience unbearable to Mom, but I digress. Back to the supermarket. When it did work, it served two purposes. First, it gave us one-on-one time that we both enjoyed and needed. Second, I was able to respond quickly—like a duck on a June bug—whenever she showed interest in any food.

> *Yes, honey, I'll be glad to buy that new, interesting-looking fruit! What's it called?*
>
> *It's, uh, a GraceFruit! Yes, a GraceFruit. It is made just for you.*
>
> *And next to it is the SillyFruit.*
>
> *Wanna see if we can make it sing?*

I would then make a big deal of feeding her the food that she had picked out. Sometimes, this even works.

In the same spirit, we have given new names to many, many foods with good results. For example, one of Grace's favorite subjects is lions. (This may have stemmed from a certain cartoon and Broadway show, but who am I to look inside the mind of another?) I actually got her to eat meat—sometime around her fourth birthday, after a great deal of resistance to the texture—by teaching her all about lions and letting her rejoice in the fact that she, too, could be a carnivore, at least part of the time. She still avoids meat when she can. This has been kind of a funny one, actually; I began to research the requirements for a healthy vegetarian diet, in part because of Grace. Most of our family now is vegetarian most of the time, and a couple of us have embraced vegetarianism whole hog (or, if you will, whole tofu).

As she gets older, I find that I worry about this less and less. She and Daddy (surprise!) enjoy the same breakfast every day. I don't just mean that they eat the same thing; I mean that both of them eat the same thing *every day.* Seven days a week. Together. Really happily. Fortunately, it's an extremely healthy breakfast.

For most meals, I either make her plate or put out the variety of food on the table and the kids can pick and choose. Some meals, she may feast exclusively on carrots and ranch or even bread with salad dressing on it, but she isn't starving, her pediatrician has no worries about it, and my days as a short-order cook are over.

As with anything else, sometimes things work that shouldn't, other things don't work that should, and some things only work for a while. When Grace was very young and only wanted bananas, I could sometimes get her to eat avocados because their texture was similar. When she was around eighteen months old, she was suddenly and irrevocably turned off by their green-ness, and that has been the end of her avocado consumption. I comfort myself with the idea that she must have eaten all of the avocados that she needed in that first year and a half, and rejoice in the fact that this leaves more guacamole for me.

One Man's Food Is Another Man's Rubbish— No Wait—It Really IS Rubbish

Sometimes, just to mix things up, my child surprises us with what she *will* eat. More on that later, but for now let's just talk about actual food. The texture and appearance of food are at least as important to your child as the taste. My child learned to like blueberries because I kept putting them in her pancakes. Now she eats them right out of her hand. (You learn to relish small victories; what can I say?) For years, I couldn't just offer her a blueberry, though. Like the restaurant waitress, I had to market: "Honey, how many plump, juicy blueberries would you like? Five or six?"

Yes, there have been times that I have given in and let her eat buttered toast for dinner, and there have been times when I have cut sandwiches with cookie cutters into shapes that she is willing to eat, and there have been times that I've announced that No, You

Can Not Have It Your Way, and kept offering what was on the menu. My "hunger is the best sauce" approach sometimes works.

My child also knows that I have a (mostly) firm policy of only having fruit as between-meal snacks, and she is reminded of this during the standoffs when she refuses to eat what is served and I don't feel like letting her have a special meal. Given the fact that she would eat dates all day long if I allowed it, I have instituted an "ask before you eat" policy for all of my kids. I have made apples available at all hours, and Grace has much more than an apple a day. (See, sometimes that desire for familiarity is helpful!)

WHAT I WISH I'D KNOWN

MY CHILD ISN'T BEING A HIGH-MAINTENANCE
EATER JUST TO ANNOY ME.
I HAVE TO BE CLEVER AND PERSISTENT ABOUT THIS.

Just a quick note here: Food can be an issue for children with ASDs, especially if parents or other caregivers make a big deal out of it. In our research, we met a boy of about eight who refused to eat anything that wasn't yellow (i.e., corn, squash, yellow M & Ms). He also refused to wear any color but yellow. He came for his evaluation in yellow sweats and a yellow t-shirt. Even his shoes were yellow. Mom said it just wasn't worth arguing with him about it. He didn't look malnourished so I'm guessing Mom was slipping in some other foods when he wasn't looking.

Many of the children I've worked with have had very limited diets. For some reason, chicken nuggets are very popular. That's baffling on several levels. A girl I saw a few times was only eating mashed potatoes and corn. Mom wasn't worried because she has a history of getting tired of the foods and moving on to another obsession. I don't know if the food limitations are part of the stereotypic behavior but I suspect it has more to do with sensory issues. Many children have told me they do not eat certain foods because of the way they feel in their mouths. Encourage your children to eat different foods and don't make mealtime a battle zone. You'll have plenty of other things to worry about. Like the following ...

Fun at the Dentist's Office

Now that we've talked about what your child puts in his mouth, let's talk about what is already in his mouth. I will warn you: embarrassment and "No, really, I'm not a bad parent!" moments are *not* limited to the park. If you haven't yet taken your little one to the dentist, let me warn you now. You will want a pediatric dentist who is willing to sedate (yes, sedate) and who is experienced with autistic children. Even so, you will want to talk with the dentist and the office staff beforehand and prepare your child. Your child may poop in his pants, even if he is a teenager. He may bite. He may flip out to such a degree that the dental visit has to be cut short. You will most likely want to have two adults on any dental visits that involve sedation. Assuming that you get as far as the dental chair, it's time for the dental exam itself. Remember all of those sweet things you put in Junior's milk so he'd get some protein? Remember all of those soft, sweet foods that he ate? Remember his refusal to let you brush or floss? It's payday. And once the dentist tells you how many cavities your child has, you will want to do your own research about the safety and efficacy of the various dental treatments and fillings available, as well as how your child will tolerate the treatment.

Toilet Paper: It's Not Just for Breakfast Anymore

Pica, as I have learned, is the practice of eating stuff that isn't food. I have also learned that it is a very common practice among kids with neurological disorders, including autism spectrum disorders. I tend to think of it as my child's immature neurological wiring taking her back to infancy for a few moments at a time. When you're a baby, you don't know that books are not food, nor are pencil erasers, or toilet paper. Just the other day, I was shooing my one-year-old away from a bowl of dog food. In his case, I expect that he'll outgrow that behavior sometime soon. In Grace's case, it resurfaces periodically, and a bit more selectively. While she won't eat some things that are, objectively, very edible, there are things that she's tried that I'm not sure I can even bring myself to tell you about.

Some People Crave Coffee

As I was trying to explain pica to a pregnant friend, she suddenly got that Eureka-I-Have-Found-It! look and said, "I know, it's like when I'm driving down the road and I suddenly have an uncontrollable craving for a milkshake!" Yes, it's like that. Except, instead of a milkshake, it's ants. Or doll toes. When you're in the throes of pica, one man's gray cardboard puzzle piece is another man's irresistible milkshake. Or so I'm told. The mother of an adolescent in Texas told me:

> *I don't trust him with Styrofoam cups.*
> *I still catch him eating notebook paper and Kleenex.*
> *He tells me it tastes good.*

As with other challenges, this one has turned us into the singingest family you've ever seen. I'm not talking musical quality here, although Grace always asks for more. She went through a time, at the age of four, when pencil erasers and the feet of dolls were her snack of choice. When she began to branch out into things that were even less appetizing, I began to appeal to Dr. DeOrnellas for help. I began to "disappear" all small magnets from the house as a precaution even though she has never eaten one of those, at least not to my knowledge.

We heard of something called a "Pica Box" (a box with stuff that's safe to chew), but were reluctant to lend any support to the consumption of stuff other than food. Plus, what the heck would I WANT to encourage her to chew? Dr. DeOrnellas, while impressed with Grace's creativity, echoed the sentiment that nobody quite knows what to do about pica, and agreed with us about the pica box. We also tried a game like "I Spy" involving food and nonfood items—we had to be equally creative! That creativity also included the creation of a song that is still a family fave and always makes them giggle:

> *Only eat your food, only eat your food,*
> *No dolls, no books, no snails, no poo,*
> *Only eat your food.*
> *Only eat your food, only eat your food,*
> *Eating dollies is not good, only eat your food.*

I should note that I try not to introduce NEW non-food items in the song. For example, if it hasn't occurred to Junior to bite his sister's magnets, the last thing I would want to do is suggest it by singing: "Your sister's magnets are not food ...." At least with my kid, that would set off an insatiable craving for magnets.

On the other hand, there is nothing wrong with being silly.

The Gift of a Cabbage Leaf

Once, at the grocery store, five-year-old Grace pulled a piece off of a head of cabbage in the produce department. I started to say, "stop," but then realized that if she'd eat it, maybe there was a solution there. I asked her, "Do you want Mommy to buy that head of cabbage?" She nodded.

I required a verbal answer: "Say 'yes, please' or 'no, thank you.'" She groaned. "No, you have to use your words. Say 'Yes, please,' or 'No, thank you.'" Eventually, I got a 'Yes, please, Mom.'"

That afternoon, we got a package from the postman that was wrapped in Styrofoam. Almost immediately, Grace attempted to nibble the Styrofoam. As I was getting it out of the house, I started thinking about that cabbage. Rather than say a word to her, since she was watching me anyway (still mesmerized by the Styrofoam), I quickly put the Styrofoam out of reach and got the cabbage out of the fridge and started washing it. Sure enough, she asked for a cabbage leaf and I was only too happy to oblige. (Okay, she reached for it and grunted and I insisted that she use her words, but it counts.) I rinsed one off and gave it to her and she happily nibbled away. Looks like we'll be keeping a head of cabbage in the refrigerator until the pica stage passes—or until she grows tired of cabbage!

Tell Me about It

One thing that worked for us—after endless rehearsal, and only for a while—was to ask Grace to come to us when she wanted to chew something. As in, "Mom! I need to chew! Now!" Mercifully, pica was not a permanent resident in our home.

Although Bobbi has managed to make pica pretty entertaining, it can be a very serious situation. Pica is a "medical condition defined as the persistent ingestion of non-nutritive substances for at least one month without an accompanying aversion to food" (Barrett, 2008, p. 1). It is not that uncommon—between ten and thirty percent of children ages one to six years have pica—but it is usually found in children with ASDs, low intelligence, developmental disabilities, and/or epilepsy (Barrett).

Children with pica eat a wide range of inedible objects, including cigarette butts, plastic toys, leaves, paint chips, paper, crayons, and erasers. Grace is the first child I have known personally to sample poo and ants but I'm sure there are others out there. Pica can be a very serious problem in some children because of the many acute medical problems that can come from it (Kern, Starosta, & Adelman, 2006). Some of the problems that have been reported are choking, infection from parasites, malnutrition, intestinal blockage or perforation, poisoning (including lead poisoning), nicotine or caffeine toxicity, surgery to remove objects, and even death (Ferreri, Tamm, & Wier 2008; Kern et al., 2006; Sturmey, Seiverling, & Ward-Horner, 2008). Sometimes children who have pica can engage in dangerous behaviors when they are looking for their preferred nonfood items or they can become aggressive if someone tries to keep them from eating the preferred item (Sturmey et al.).

The cause of pica is unknown but several theories have been proposed. One is that the child has a poor diet with resulting deficiencies in minerals and other nutrients (Barrett, 2008). Since making sure children with ASDs eat nutritiously can be so difficult, vitamin deficiencies are a possibility. Some children with pica have a genetic disorder (i.e., Prader-Willi). In some cases, the neurotransmission of dopamine is deficient or serotonin levels are elevated. Some believe that pica originates when children imitate a family pet while others consider pica another form of stereotypic behavior. In any case, pica may continue because the child obtains positive reinforcement in the form of attention from adult caregivers or from the reinforcing sensory experience of chewing (Barrett).

Does your child have it? Possibly, maybe even probably. All children with ASDs should be evaluated for pica. Observable symptoms include vomiting, nausea, pale or flushed appearance, gagging, and/or lethargy (Ferreri et al., 2008). The evaluation process begins with an interview of the parents and any of the child's siblings. Frequently, siblings will know about pica when parents do not (Barrett, 2008). In addition to an interview, a complete physical examination should be conducted that includes lab studies to detect toxic substances such as lead, mercury, or copper, and to rule out dietary deficiencies. Liver function tests and electrolyte measurements should also be included. In some cases, diagnostic imaging may be required to determine if objects that cannot be digested or obstructive masses are present in the digestive system (Barrett).

Preventing pica is the most effective form of treatment. For children who are driven to eat non-food items due to anxiety or obsessive-compulsive behavior, a trial of SSRI (selective serotonin reuptake inhibitor) antidepressants may be indicated. For other children, behavior modification or a combination of behavior modification and medication may be helpful (Barrett, 2008). However, for many children with pica, the condition is very difficult to treat. As previously noted, the act of chewing is very reinforcing to some children and the oral stimulation they receive maintains the behavior (Kern et al., 2006).

One method of treatment that has shown limited promise is the substitution of edible foods for inedible foods (Kern et al., 2006). Foods such as popcorn can be substituted for plastic toys (or whatever the child is eating that is not meant to be consumed). Published studies have shown some success in using an exchange system for a limited time (i.e., five to ten minutes). Problems noted with this technique have included limited effectiveness across settings, satiation, and a lack of dietary balance (Kern et al.). For example, the child with pica is willing to trade the toy for popcorn until they are too full to continue eating popcorn, and a diet of popcorn is not balanced or particularly nutritious. In addition, the child may exchange the toy for popcorn in a very controlled setting, such as the preschool class, but not on the playground or in the grocery store (Kern et al.).

Ferreri et al. (2006) were able to decrease pica significantly in a four-year-old boy diagnosed with autism in a preschool setting. The boy chewed the appendages of plastic figures and was suffering from physical complications as a result. Ferreri and colleagues determined the boy had a food aversion to tapioca pudding so they dipped the toys in tapioca pudding before putting them out in the room. When given the opportunity to play with the treated toys, the boy tasted them and did not try to eat them. Eventually, the toys no longer had to be treated and the boy played with them without mouthing or chewing them. This behavior continued into the next school year.

> That said, I think Bobbi is on to something. By being vigilant and catching the early warning signs that Grace needs to chew something, and then substituting real food, she seems to be making progress. This method beats some of the other techniques I've heard—such as having individuals wear fencing masks so they cannot ingest non-edibles. This technique is punishing rather than instructive and does not change the behavior. And most of us don't have fencing masks lying around.

Our Own Personal Food Pyramid

As with any other issue, there are things that work for a time and there are things that don't work at all. One thing that we tried was to make a poster with pictures of what she will eat and make a game of adding things to it. When she has something in her mouth, I can say, "Look at the poster. Is that food?" That worked for a while. Now, not so much.

I also praise her for eating actual food, especially if it's something that she hasn't eaten before. When doing so, I often have to remember to join my child in her world, and not demand that it be the other way around. Let me give an example. Recently, we made the houses for the Three Little Pigs. It was a messy, yummy project involving graham crackers, shredded wheat, pretzels, and other items. (Suddenly, it's making sense that my child doesn't distinguish between food and non-food. Wait a minute ....)

Since the Three Pigs project, she will sometimes eat a bowl of shredded wheat cereal. However, if I refer to what she is eating as "cereal," "food," or any other term that makes sense to me, she won't eat it. Instead, we have to discuss the *straw* that she is eating from *Piggie Lucy's house*. Works like a charm. Now I just have to figure out a way to slip a steak and a salad into the cereal bowl. Actually, I have gotten a lot of inspiration from *Deceptively Delicious* by Jessica Seinfeld. After reading that book, I'm sneaking pureed squash into the mac & cheese and plotting my next cake. I think I'm brave enough to slip in some beets.

Garbage In, Garbage Out

I have become very, very aware of what goes into my child's body, whether it is food, medication, or even what she breathes. Being a mother has made me crunchy and green in ways I couldn't have imagined a decade ago, and dealing with autism spectrum issues has only made this more true.

You may not realize that I'm right on the edge of some very treacherous waters here. Parents who care passionately about their children may become reasonably convinced that environmental toxins, dairy products, vaccines, or gluten are the cause of their child's difficulties, and I am not here to argue with any of them. *I have to say that again:* I am not here to dispute anyone who has found the key to what causes or heals their child's difficulties. On the contrary, if you are reading this and you have found something that is working—or that may work—you have only my admiration and support. Also, you're right. I've been telling you to trust yourself, haven't I? Besides, you don't have to have a child on the autism spectrum to have very, very strong opinions about your kid's diet.

You are going to have to educate yourself and form your own opinions, and, as with so many other things about the autism spectrum, there is a wide range of opinions about what will hurt or what will help. I encourage you to listen with an open mind and really observe your child.

You are going to have to figure this out for yourself, and it may take years. I am not a doctor. I don't even play one on TV. My personal experience is that there are enough autistic-like behaviors on both sides of our family that I am convinced that much of what my child experienced would have happened no matter what pesticides we used. As far as I can tell, my daughter's autism is not the regressive type.

Having said that, if I had to do it all over again, I would have jumped on the organic bandwagon much, much sooner, and I would have scrutinized every single vaccine and medication that was administered to her. I can say, with certainty, that my child does much better when she has at least two hours of vigorous exercise each day, gets a good, uninterrupted night's sleep, watches as few videos as possible, gets time to herself when she needs it, has a lot of cuddling, and eats a minimum of processed food. You are going to have to figure this out for yourself, and the Bibliography section provides at least a starting point to the best-known approaches.

Wouldn't we all do better with Bobbi's prescription for health: at least two hours of vigorous exercise each day; a good, uninterrupted night's sleep; watching as few videos (or TV) as possible; time to herself when she needs it; a lot of cuddling; and a minimum of processed food?

Sweet Dreams

Mercifully, I have little to contribute to this particular discussion. I understand that sleep problems can be major in children with ASDs. In our case, Grace's sleep pattern has been unusual, but not really problematic; she sleeps like a rock through the night and she does not nap. Even from early infancy, she was very resistant to sleeping during the day. I have heard other parents say that the refusal to nap, even when the child is obviously tired, is part of the sensory issues—failing to appreciate that sleep is what she needs—and unwillingness to break her focus from the activities of the day.

For us, this has been okay because she does sleep so well at night. She is the only child I know who consistently goes to bed willingly. Sometimes, she'll quietly slip off to bed, and other times, she'll make an announcement and demand lullabies.

We did have some challenges about *where* she slept. We have had some bouts of hysteria when beloved items could not be found at bedtime. She also does not welcome any changes to her bed. Since she likes small, cave-like spaces, we found her a tot bed that is in the shape of a small car, with a plastic sunroof/canopy. She loved it. When she outgrew it, we went through several nylon bed tents before we found one that she didn't destroy (thank you, IKEA). We wracked our brains and tried lots of alternatives, including a twin bed, a mattress on the floor, and sharing a large bed with her sisters. Had the bunk with the tent not worked, I guess we'd have to consider letting her sleep in the closet. That would freak me out just a little, but I think she'd love it.

I had to laugh when I read that Bobbi was considering a bed in the closet for Grace. My own daughter, who is not on the spectrum and is successfully grown, slept on a shelf we put in her closet when she was Grace's age. It was actually sort of a loft arrangement and she had a twin-size mattress but she loved it.

Although Grace does not have sleep problems, many children with ASDs do. This has been true for a number of the children and adolescents that I work with. Parents have expressed concern that their children have difficulty falling asleep, that they wake in the middle of the night, and that their children wander around the house during the night. In 1989, Konstantareas and Homatidis reported that sleep problems were the number one management problem of parents of children on the spectrum (cited in Goodlin-Jones, Tang, Liu, & Anders, 2008) and numerous other studies have described the stress sleep problems cause for parents. Several researchers have looked at the extent of sleep problems in children with ASDs. Allik, Larsson, and Smedje found that children with HFASD had more trouble falling asleep than typically developing children (2006). In a study of preschoolers with ASD, developmental delay without autism, and typical development, the children with ASD slept less in 24 hours than the other two groups of children (Goodlin-Jones et al.).

Insomnia is the most frequently reported sleep disorder for children with ASD. Insomnia in children is defined as "repeated difficulty with sleep initiation, duration, consolidation, or quality that occurs despite age-appropriate time and opportunity for sleep and results in daytime functional impairment for the child and/or family" (Johnson & Malow, 2008, p. 774).

Johnson and Malow go on to explain various causes of insomnia in children with ASDs. Among the possibilities are a coexisting neurological disorder (such as epilepsy), insufficient nighttime melatonin production, a coexisting medical disorder (such as gastrointestinal reflux disease), poor sleep hygiene, a coexisting psychiatric disorder (such as anxiety), medications that are being taken for coexisting disorders (including asthma, ADHD, depression, or anxiety), and other sleep disorders. Another possible cause is behavioral in nature. It occurs when parents encourage poor sleep habits. For example, rocking your child to sleep and then putting him in bed solves the initial problem of getting him to sleep but will have to be repeated when he wakes up in the middle of the night.

Obstructive sleep apnea (OSA) is another cause of sleep problems in children. It is characterized by loud breathing, snoring, restless sleep, and sweating (Johnson & Malow, 2008). Instead of being sleepy during the day, as most adults with OSA are, children are more likely to be hyperactive and have other problem behaviors. Tonsillectomy and ade-noidectomy are usually the first choice of treatment.

If your child is having trouble sleeping, take a good look at your own behaviors first and make sure you aren't inadvertently causing sleep problems. If not, check with your child's pediatrician.

Potty Training:
Developmental Delays Can Get Disgusting

There are behaviors that are confusing (like "stimming"), and there are behaviors that are scary (like cliff-diving from shelves), and then there are behaviors that are confusing, scary, and just plain appalling. Yuck. For a variety of reasons ranging from sensory issues to developmental immaturity, many kids on the autism spectrum—and some who aren't—take their time in learning to use the toilet.

My completely non-scientific survey has revealed that it is not at all uncommon for ASD kids to potty-train around the age of five. Yes, I said five. Or older. You should also understand that the term "potty-trained" may have incremental definitions that aren't exactly what you'd hoped. (Now would be the time to set this book down and weep before continuing.) That would be consistent with our experience (as would the weeping). We joke that my next book should be *Potty Train Your Child in Ten Years or Less*, closely followed by *Lose Five Pounds in Ten Years*. I had friends who thought that we were done simply because we couldn't bring ourselves to talk about it anymore. Your child may be five or older before he begins to even show the basic signs of potty training readiness. When your friends tell you about those awful weeks when they pushed the potty-training to conclusion and then cleaned the carpets, just make a mental note to substitute "years" for "weeks" in that sentence, and you'll be fine.

You should also understand the challenge of transferability of skills. Home is not the same as Not Home. Night is not the same as day. There may be a differential of years between being able to go #1 in the potty and #2 in the potty.

BEN SAYS

MANY OF THE THINGS THAT BOBBI WRITES ABOUT
DON'T REALLY BOTHER ME, BUT THE POO THING?
NOW *THAT* ... *THAT* WAS A TRIAL.

If your child has sensory issues, you may learn not to think of potty training as an event. When our kids are overwhelmed—and remember, things may overwhelm them that wouldn't even faze you because some of their senses are turned way, way up—they may let you know with things other than words. Our kids aren't necessarily tuned in to hygiene the way that we are, and *they aren't doing this to annoy us.* I can tell you candidly that my husband and I find this very, very trying. We have to remind ourselves—and one another—that this is *not,* I repeat, *not* something that she is doing to annoy us. One of the hardest things about parenting a child with an autism spectrum disorder is stepping back from the frustration of the moment and recognizing what is a discipline issue and what is a training issue. If you can separate these things consistently, give me a call. If you're human, you're going to make some mistakes. Hopefully, I've convinced you that you aren't the only parent of a four-, five-, or even twelve-year-old who hasn't got the potty thing down yet:

> *Oh, my goodness!! Potty training with him was a nightmare!! He was about 6 1/2 before I could FINALLY say he is completely potty trained! He had many, many an accident even though I was sure he knew what, how, when to go potty. I eventually started making him clean his own messes. I had to stop making him clean out his own underwear when one day he accidentally flushed a pair down the toilet! Daddy had to take the toilet apart to fish them out.*
>
> — D., FLORIDA

So, what worked? We did work with Dr. DeOrnellas on some behavioral modification—stuff that is going to be totally specific to each child in terms of what is aversive and what is motivating, but mostly I think she just decided to try using the potty. Sometimes we'd have days—or even weeks—of success. Then again, when she was four, she once pulled off the fitted sheet, tore a hole in the plastic mattress cover, replaced the sheet, and peed in that spot. When I asked her why (please don't imagine me doing so in a calm manner), she said (in a very calm manner), "I was making a nest." (Huh?)

Having a younger sibling who is potty training may also be a help, but don't bet on it. Everyone said that having a younger sibling was going to motivate Grace to potty-train. However, Everyone clearly didn't understand that a kid with Asperger's is really not competitive or tuned in to peer pressure. Although I wouldn't say it was a motivator, they surely did bond over their favorite potty video. (Elmo, if you're reading this, I know all of your songs.)

Are you ready for some good news? We don't have the hubris to actually own a banner that says "Mission Accomplished," but she is a Big Girl Now. Please excuse me while I take a break from writing and weep for joy.

FROM BEN—
WHAT I WISH I'D KNOWN

GOD HELP US, WE STILL DON'T KNOW.

Somehow, Bobbi has managed to make this one of the funnier chapters in this book. However, I can tell you this has not always been a humorous topic for her—and I would venture to say that Ben has yet to find the humor in it. Potty training Grace was a frequent topic in my sessions with the Sheahan family and, despite being raised on a farm, Ben was particularly disgusted by the creative uses Grace found for feces.

Grace is not unusual in her resistance to toilet training and, while most children are trained during the day and have incidents of bedwetting at night, her reversal of the process was confusing to me. While searching through the recent literature on autism spectrum disorders, I was surprised to find very little on toilet training. Apparently, even the experts are reluctant to tackle this topic. One of the most helpful books I found was *Toilet Training for Individuals with Autism or other Developmental Issues* by Maria Wheeler. She describes factors related to toilet training, discusses the problems for families and the individual when toilet training is not accomplished in a timely manner, and walks the reader (presumably a parent or teacher) through the process. This is accomplished in an easy-to-read style with case examples to help you remember this is a common problem.

Before we discuss the process of toilet training, it is important to know the lingo. The first is enuresis. Enuresis refers to urination in inappropriate places. In order to be diagnosed, it must occur repetitively and after the chronological (or mental) age of four years. It cannot be the result of a general medical condition or a substance (such as a diuretic). Enuresis can occur during the day (diurnal) or at night (nocturnal) and it has been related to poor toilet training, underdeveloped bladders, and stressful situations.

The second term is encopresis. Encopresis is having repeated bowel movements in inappropriate places, such as in clothing, beds, etc.). Like enuresis, encopresis occurs after the age of four, and is not the result of taking laxatives or other substances or a general medical condition. It can be voluntary or involuntary and may or may not be accompanied by constipation. Is has been related to poor toilet training and stress.

Encopresis has been a problem for a number of children and adolescents with whom I have worked and it always seems to be more distressing for the family than for the individual. It can be very difficult and confusing to treat because it sometimes reflects children's need to control something in their lives. For example, the child who feels he has no say in what happens to him may try to find some control in where and when he defecates. As a result, we see children who only have bowel movements in their clothing at school or on the way home from school. Years ago, I worked with a family that was so chaotic and out of control that I dreaded each session. The six-year-old boy was the "identified patient" because he was encopretic at home. It did not take long to understand that he was reacting to the chaos. Once the grown-ups began to cooperate and establish a routine at home, the encopresis disappeared.

Enuresis and encopresis are both attributed to stressful situations. For children with ASDs, much of the world is a stressful situation—whether we are aware of the stress or not. Establishing routines for toileting is very important. Not making a crisis out of each toileting accident is equally important. Nevertheless, this is a very difficult situation for families and their children.

Wheeler (2007) discusses the difficulty of toilet training the child with ASD and encourages parents to keep in mind the following child-related factors: "communication needs, literal communication, sensory awareness, sensitivity to stimulation, preference for routine or ritual, motor planning difficulties, limited imitation, sequential learning, increased levels of anxiety, and difficulty adjusting behaviors to fit new situations" (p. 2). Being able to successfully toilet has far-reaching implications for the child and the family. Children who are not toilet trained by the time they enter elementary school are subject to ridicule from peers and irritation from teachers. Choosing not to toilet train and relying instead on diapers is a disservice to your child if he or she is physically capable of being trained. Using picture schedules and/or Social Stories are effective methods of toilet training. Breaking it down into steps will be required. Mentally walk yourself through the steps involved in toileting and use pictures or a story to represent each step so your child will know what is expected. Don't forget to incorporate hand washing as part of the routine.

Habit training is an option for those children who do not recognize when they have a wet diaper or have the urge to urinate or defecate. Habit training involves taking the child to the bathroom at set intervals, after meals, before and after a nap, etc. If you are using a picture schedule, there should be numerous potty breaks throughout the day. Eventually, your child will begin to toilet independently and achieve continence. However, some children never seem to make the connection between staying dry and toileting.

Toilet training is one of the first efforts we make at teaching our children to take care of their personal hygiene needs. Unfortunately, for many parents, teaching or enforcing self-care is difficult. Older children and adolescents (even some adults) with ASD often neglect their grooming.

Getting these individuals to brush their teeth, bathe, wash or brush their hair, or wear clean clothing can be a constant struggle. Individuals with ASD may seem oblivious to their own odors and to the reactions of others around them. Establishing these habits at an early age is necessary to help our children avoid further stigmatization. Parents need to enforce rules regarding using deodorant and wearing clean socks and underwear. Girls also must be taught to take care of their hygiene during menstruation. Each year, parents of children with ASD are hit with new challenges and the same tools that worked in the past (picture schedules and Social Stories) may continue to be effective. Some families I know tie completing personal hygiene activities to reward systems. For example, showering and putting on deodorant can be exchanged for a certain amount of computer time. As usual, whatever works for someone else's child may not work for yours and what worked for your child today may not work tomorrow. Remain steadfast and flexible.

The Feng Shui of Autism Spectrum Disorders

Regardless of my approach to a particular behavior, I have become a champ at novel childproofing. I once had a friend jokingly refer to our Asperger's-proofed house as "Maximum Security Manor." In my case, this included getting rid of small toys that are choking hazards and asking myself if board books were really friend or foe (recall the discussion of pica).

I don't think that it's possible to exaggerate Grace's capacity to lay waste to a living space. She can make a mess in three minutes that takes three days and a steam cleaner to clean up.

BEN AND BOBBI SAY

YOU KNOW HOW YOUR TODDLER CLIMBS
ON THE TABLE AND TRASHES STUFF?
JUST DON'T EXPECT THAT TO END, AND YOU'LL BE FINE.

One day, I asked Grace, "What makes Mommy and Daddy sad?" and she said, "Destruction." She was five; she'd heard that word a few times. Fortunately, I can relate that some of that abated by age seven. So, what do we do to survive the destruction? If a behavior is merely immature, then we can:

- Try approaching it as we would with a younger child, which mostly consists of repetition and prevention, and

- Watch to see if she's just going to grow out of it.

Actually, I'm going to add one to that list.

- Instead of assuming that Grace wants to destroy our house, can I consider that this is sensory-seeking behavior?

BEN SAYS

WHO THE HELL CARES WHY? TELL HER TO STOP.

Lots of visual cues and reminders are in the home. I try to create organizers for areas that require logical sequence.

— J., CALIFORNIA

I am especially jealous of S. in Oklahoma, who went to the trouble of:

changing our living room into a sensory room with swing suspended from the ceiling and crash mat on the floor.

We could all use that sometimes, couldn't we?

I can also speculate that this may also be nothing more than a developmental delay. When Grace was six, she was able to exercise tremendous self-control around her sister's birthday cake. This was greatly appreciated by her sister, and would not have been possible even a few months earlier.

Locks That Are Child-Proof, Adult-Proof, Idiot-Proof—Even Burglar-Proof!

Grace had two unfortunate bouts with running away at ages three and five. I don't mean sophisticated, pack-a-suitcase running away; I mean running off headlong like a toddler. I was overjoyed on the day that she encountered an open backyard gate and stood there, transfixed, and finally said to me, "Mommy, I stayed in the yard." She was six and a half. I still puddle up when I think of this conversation.

We found a childproofing company that not only successfully kept Grace indoors, but had a hidden benefit as well. These locks, which are not immediately visible unless you know what you're looking for, were installed on all of our exterior doors as well as some of our interior doors. I knew that I had really gotten my money's worth on the day that a burglar attempted to break into our house. Although he managed to defeat both the usual locks on our front door, he could not get our front door open because of the childproof locks. True story. That's some kind of lock, I said. Childproof, Asperger's-proof, and even burglar proof!

I Need My Space. Really.

When I say that having an ASD in the family will rearrange your life, I am speaking both literally and figuratively. In our case, we have lots of little spaces in our house and yard that Grace can squeeze into. Sometimes, this means that we have to play "Find-the-Grace," but it gives comfort to curl up in certain cabinets or that little space between the tree and the fence. Our backyard includes lots of "hiding" places and trees that can be (sort of) safely climbed, and—of course—a swing set.

Physical Activity = Medicine

My prescription for sanity for me and my kids centers around some really sophisticated concepts like getting enough sleep (a task at which I generally fail), moving a lot, and being outdoors whenever we can. Instead of a formal dining room, we have a room with a craft table, a mini-trampoline, a spinning disc, and several hippity hops.

BEN SAYS

WHERE'S THE DINING ROOM TABLE?

Please don't get the idea that I just take all of what we'll generally—and euphemistically—call "Grace's sensory seeking behavior" in stride. Oh, no. I once dissolved into tears upon seeing the waste that she had laid to the linen closet. Yes, I was embarrassed afterwards that I overreacted to some unfolded sheets and towels—and they didn't even have her favorite "brown crayon" treatment—but we're talking a LOT of sheets and towels. These instances provide the opportunity for lengthy arguments with the voices in my head (or is that my husband?) about whether this behavior is naughtiness or "sensory stuff" and how I ought to respond (other than crying, I mean). The truth is, *it doesn't really matter.*

WHAT I WISH I'D KNOWN

I AM NOT GOING TO TALK MY DAUGHTER OUT
OF THESE BEHAVIORS, NOR SHOULD I TREAT
THEM LIKE NAUGHTINESS. I STILL CAN'T ALWAYS
FIND THAT LINE, BUT AT LEAST I KNOW TO LOOK FOR IT.

Having Grace participate in cleaning up the mess is important whether she *meant* to destroy the afternoon or not. It's just a reality. Talking with her about what we should and should not do is a necessity either way. In the instance of the linens, my initial impression—that it was naughtiness—was befuddled by the fact that she spent much of the rest of the day rolling herself up in an enormous roll of paper that we use for artsy stuff on a good day. It was clear to me that something about the crunchy noise, the rolly-ness, the wrapped-up-itude, really spoke to her soul. So, was the destruction of the linen closet preschool vandalism or just the scratching of a sensory itch? Probably both.

REFERENCES:

Allik, H., Larsson, J-O., & Smedje, H. (2006). Sleep patterns of school-age children with Asperger's syndrome or high-functioning autism. *Journal of Autism and Developmental Disorders, 36*, 585–595.

American Psychological Association. (2007). *APA dictionary of psychology.* Washington, DC: Author.

Barrett, R. P. (2008). Pica: Toward understanding a complicated condition. *The Brown University Child and Adolescent Behavior Letter, 24*(6), 1, 5–6.

Ferreri, S. J., Tamm, L., & Wier, K. G. (2006). Using food aversion to decrease severe pica by a child with autism. *Behavior Modification, 30*, 456–471.

Goodlin-Jones, B. L., Tang, K., Liu, J., & Anders, T. F. (2008). Sleep patterns in preschool-age children with autism, developmental delay, and typical development. *Journal of the American Academy of Child and Adolescent Psychiatry, 47*(8), 930–938.

Johnson, K. P., & Malow, B. A. (2008). Assessment and pharmacologic treatment of sleep disturbance in autism. *Child and Adolescent Psychiatric Clinics of North America, 17*, 773–785.

Kern, L., Starosta, K. & Adelman, B. E. (2006). Reducing pica by teaching children to exchange inedible items for edibles. *Behavior Modification, 30*, 135–158.

Sheridan, K. & Raffield, T. (2008). Teaching adaptive skills to people with autism. In J. Matson, (Ed.), *Clinical assessment and intervention for autism spectrum disorders* (pp. 327–350). Burlington, MA: Elsevier Press.

Sturmey, P., Seiverling, L., & Ward-Horner, J. (2008). Assessment of challenging behaviors in people with autism spectrum disorders. In J. Matson (Ed.), *Clinical assessment and intervention for autism spectrum disorders* (pp. 131–163). Burlington, MA: Academic Press.

Wheeler, M. (2007). *Toilet training for individuals with autism or other developmental issues.* Arlington, TX: Future Horizons.

CHAPTER SIX

My Kid, She's Not Much of a Talker

Our children have all kinds of "issues" when it comes to talking, whether it's too much talking, talking that makes no sense to us, or no talking at all. Grace started late and her speech was atypical.

Our son spoke his first SENTENCE when he was just over 3 years old.

— A., Minnesota

That's a familiar story to me. Once the sentences start, they can grow into paragraphs, with no indication that your child has the foggiest notion of what he's saying. Should we be proud of our children's powers of memory and recitation? That is a hard question to answer when you have no idea what your child is trying to really say. It is frustrating in the extreme when we don't understand our own children.

Echolalia, which you may recall from the movie, *Rain Man*, is the practice of repeating what a speaker has said, sometimes over and over, rather than responding. Delayed echolalia, which is, in my experience, more common, is what my daughter Lucy and some of her friends call "TV talk" or "movie talk"; in other words, I think that I'm having a conversation with my child and only belatedly realize that she is quoting something that she saw in a video or heard from a book.

My child's excessive quoting and memorizing has receded as her communication skills have increased, but she will still drop a line—or several—from a song, a story, or a movie. Now she actually uses them appropriately, as opposed to just quoting non sequiturs. I should add a warning here: quoting back draws mixed results. If I have quoted inaccurately, she may find this very upsetting. If I quote accurately, I may find myself drawn into a very vivid role-playing game as I'm changing lanes on the highway. Eventually, we learned to leverage this behavior. There are excellent books and videos out there for our kids, including a DVD series called *Model Me Kids* and several books by Cheri Meiners, M.Ed. with titles like *Be Polite and Kind* and *Join in and Play*. We also appreciated *Hands are not for Hitting,* by Martine Agassi, Ph.D. These books and DVDs have been very helpful with everything from language development and playdates to how to handle a transition between activities.

As Grace's language skills have grown, she has retained her tendency to quote, but the quotes are now (mostly) appropriate to the situation and delivered in context. For example, if her book says, "Hands are not for hitting," she may state this line, in the exact tone that it was read to her, in response to being smacked by her sister. I should warn you—this line might be delivered in conjunction with hitting back.

She can also be rigid about the use of words and phrases. Our children are very literal. Yes, I realize that all children are literal, especially when they are very young, but our kids' view of language isn't flexible or playful. For the same reasons that she didn't babble or experiment with consonant sounds as a baby, Grace doesn't now play with words. When Grace was six, she announced to us that she wanted to become a nun. (She had previously been telling us that she wanted to be a baker, a soldier, a veterinarian, and/or the mother of many children, so I wouldn't start measuring her for a habit just yet.) The family had been listing flower names that could also be used on humans, so I playfully asked her if she wanted to be named Sister Daffodil. She sternly rebuked me, telling me that she would need "a Nunnish name." If you think that your child is going to understand metaphors, wordplay, or puns, you'd better think again. You or a sibling may think that something is funny, and Junior will not share that opinion. I was actually highly impressed that she was able to analyze and process my name suggestion and quickly respond. A year or two ago, she wouldn't have had that skill.

Speaking of language and our kids' relationship to language, I highly recommend that you teach idioms to your children as if they are a second language. My husband and I have had a lot of fun with this because, even though English is his first language, he grew up in another culture. He likes to say, "We are separated by our common language."

The *Amelia Bedelia* series by Peggy Parish are a wonderful way to introduce your children to idioms and figures of speech in a humorous way. There are entire books full of idioms. Remember, our kids are very visual and very literal; idioms can really trip them up. My friend Elizabeth Scott read and explained an idiom a day to her son Roman, and she explained to me how helpful this has been; now, when someone says, "It's raining cats and dogs," Roman will look at her and say, "Mom, that's an idiom. It means that it's raining very hard." Cheri J. Meiners is the author of several books, including *Understand and Care* and *Be Polite and Kind*. These books have wonderful illustrations and have been especially helpful to us. They give children not only the framework, but also the vocabulary for both social skills and empathy. One of Grace's favorite books is *The Way I Feel* by Janan Cain, because it gives short, rhyming descriptions of various emotions with hilarious, exaggerated illustrations. Joy Berry has also authored a wonderful series with titles like *Let's Talk About Being Helpful* and *Let's Talk About Feeling Sad.*

WHAT I WISH I'D KNOWN

SOMETIMES, ALL THAT'S NECESSARY
IS A LITTLE TRANSLATION.

Call Unto Me and I Will Answer Thee
(Jeremiah 33:3)

We've talked about the confusion that can occur when our kids talk to us; what about when they won't? A technique that has worked well for us is to require our daughter to verbalize, even when we know what she wants. This requires a huge amount of patience from Mom and Dad, but it's worth it. When she was four, Grace would whine and pull at the pantry door to let me know she wanted her favorite snack. When she is talking unintelligibly, or using non-word groans and pulling me towards the swing, I pretty much know that she wants me to push her. I require, kindly and firmly, that she verbalize her request, complete with The Magic Word—please!—before I will perform for her. At the age of six, she tried to answer questions by using only the first letter of the word she intended to use. It took a great deal of persuasion to make her understand that this was not going to be an efficient way to communicate.

This also works the other way around. When I am trying to get her attention, I have been known to say such brilliant things as, "Listen to me with your *face*," as I get right in front of her. When I give her an instruction, I require her to either repeat back what she is going to do or give me a "Yes, Mom." This sets the wheels of compliance in motion before she even realizes it.

Please don't think that you are supposed to be a saint. Your patience is being tried. And tried. And tried. Once you get your child's attention, you may need to break the simplest task down to pieces that are so much smaller than bite-sized. I recently surprised one of my relatives by describing our five-month effort to teach Grace how to grip a pencil. Seeing things through his eyes was, well, very eye-opening for me. Sometimes we get so busy with our struggles that we don't give ourselves credit for the challenges we are surmounting every day. It is very, very frustrating for your child to blow you off, whether he's hyper-focusing or merely ignoring you. The fact that your child has an autism spectrum disorder is an explanation, not an excuse. Requiring your child to be in the habit of listening to you will save you both a lot of grief. As with other things, it is two steps forward, one step back (or two or three or four). For us, progress comes in fits and starts. Grace's Uncle John, who hadn't seen her in a year, remarked that he was amazed at her progress in conversation, eye contact, and compliance, and that she seemed to him to be a "completely different child." Such reports are a reality check. A good, welcome, encouraging reality check. Getting lost in the day-to-day struggles can blind you to the miracles that have happened over the weeks or the months.

WHAT I WISH I'D KNOWN

I WISH I'D KEPT A JOURNAL OF
GRACE'S PROGRESS SO THAT I COULD REFER TO IT
ON THE DAYS WHEN I WAS REALLY DISCOURAGED.

Ask Me No Questions and I'll Tell You No Lies

You may find that asking your child a question is like talking to the cat. Allow me to condense a year and a half of language lessons.

If I ask: *"Honey, how are you feeling?"*

I'm probably not going to be acknowledged at all. Let's try that again. *"Honey, are you sad?"*

Nope, still doesn't even look up.

"Honey, what do you need?" Still, I'm sucking wind.

Listen to Me with Your Face

Okay, let's approach this from a different angle. First, I have to get right in front of my child and make sure that she makes eye contact with me. This may be easy to do or difficult, depending on the level of your child's resistance. My child has learned to respond to the following questions and command, which must be stated verbatim:

"[Child's name], do not ignore Mommy/are you ignoring me?"
and
"Listen to me with your FACE."

Once I have her attention, I have to ask the correct question. My experience cross-examining and taking depositions has stood me in good stead here. When you've asked a hostile witness, "Where did you graduate?" and been told: "In the auditorium," you learn to be very specific. I find that giving her alternatives that she understands is helpful. Instead of asking if she needs to be alone or feels anxious, I will give two very concrete alternatives:

"Do you want your sister to come in here,
or will I shut the door?"

She will usually indicate one or the other, at which point, kindly but firmly, I require a verbal response. "No, you have to say either 'come' or 'shut door,' honey," at which point she will parrot one of those two.

Multitasking? Uh, No.

Like many moms, I am a multitasker to a fault. I can fix dinner, do my nails, check my email, and play a board game with one child while changing another child's diaper. (Ew.) My husband, on the other hand, does one thing at a time. He does one thing at a time very well, mind you, but seriously only one thing at a time. For this reason, he understood before I did that I couldn't expect Grace to carry on a conversation with me while I was brushing her hair. For Grace, having her hair brushed was a full-body and full-mind experience that eliminated the possibility of other conversations.

BEN'S COMMENT

OF COURSE SHE CAN'T DO ANYTHING ELSE
WHILE YOU'RE BRUSHING HER HAIR!
HONEY, WHAT ARE YOU THINKING?

This One Thing At A Time Principle also explains why my daughter loves books on CD. She can devote all of her attention to listening, unlike a video or even having Mommy read to her (both of which she loves, but it's a different experience). We have fallen into a rhythm of listening to books on CD in the car, which is perfect because it usually precedes or follows something that's overstimulating to her (a trip to the grocery store, the zoo, someone's house, you name it), and so the downtime is essential. You aren't limited to your child's reading (or pre-reading) level, either. We listen to kids' stories, history, chapter books, and music. If a sibling is in a play, Grace is a tremendous help. I mean, think about it. What could be better than having your little sister memorize the script and score almost instantly? And she never gets tired of the repetition. No joke.

A paradoxical thing about this is that my little hyper-focuser is also sometimes highly distractible. Temple Grandin, in her magnificent *Animals in Translation*, explains how an autistic person can't ignore things that you and I can "filter out," like the sound of a truck backing up or a cell phone ringing. Grace cannot bear the scary Halloween displays in stores or in our neighbors' yards; they are literally painful to her, and she cannot turn away. She is very, very vocal about her objections, and I have had to run a little interference (and alter our route home during the month of October) because our neighbors really are wonderful, and it's not their fault that Grace has an outsize reaction to their décor and cannot turn away. I no longer take my ability to shift focus for granted; this insight is one of the gifts of being Grace's parent.

It's Raining Cats and Dogs

Speaking of speech, in case you haven't already figured this out, our kids do NOT "get" metaphors, similes, and figures of speech. There are entire books written on this subject, but you may find that your child isn't responding or obeying because you're using the wrong words. If I told my daughter to "hop to it," she would either literally *hop* or (more likely) ignore me because hopping would not make sense to her in the situation.

WHAT I WISH I'D KNOWN

OUR KIDS AREN'T IGNORING US ON PURPOSE,
NOR ARE THEY TRYING TO AGGRAVATE US.
(WELL, NOT ANY MORE THAN ANY OTHER KID.)
THEIR INABILITY TO SHIFT FOCUS AT WILL CAN BE
AS ANNOYING TO OUR KIDS AS IT IS TO US.
WE CAN GET THEIR ATTENTION, JUST IN DIFFERENT
WAYS THAN WE WOULD WITH ANOTHER KID.

Sometimes, frustration really does give birth to progress. On a recent day, when my children and I had not been bringing out the best in one another (see how nice I made that sound? I wanted to sell them to the zoo), I tried something in my frustration that has become a terrific tool. Since Grace has a hard time responding verbally to questions, I placed her across the room from me and asked her yes-and-no questions. I instructed her to take one step towards me for each "yes" answer. Without even being told, she took a step away from me for each "no" answer. I had some specific information that I wanted from her, but I hadn't been getting anywhere by trying to talk with her (go figure). I managed to include lots of silly questions to get her giggling—Are you married? Are you a chicken? Is your name Boogashmoo?—and she was so engrossed in the physical tasks of step-taking that she answered my "real" questions without even realizing that they were part of the game.

I could have chosen to be frustrated that I had to jump through hoops to get simple information, but it's really about reaching and loving your child where she is. I had to remind myself that it really is the same communication; it's just a different language. This is just one more way that we have to reach around the disability to get to our child. Speaking of language, this is as good a place as any to encourage you to tell your child every day, several times a day, that he is wonderful just the way he is and that you love and enjoy him. Even though he may not seem to respond to you, it's going to change *you* when you hear yourself say those words day after day. Plus, repetition often works wonders with our kids, and they need a connection with us even though they don't seem to want it. All of the "discipline" in the world isn't going to matter if your child doesn't know that you love him—however he understands love.

WHAT I WISH I'D KNOWN

THE TOOLS THAT WORK WITH MY OTHER KIDS—
YOU KNOW, THINGS LIKE TALKING, REASONING, AND HUGGING—
WILL BE A DISASTER WHEN I TRY THEM ON GRACE. IT'S BACK TO
THE DRAWING BOARD—AND MOSTLY, I FOLLOW HER LEAD.

As we discussed in Autism 101, a delay in developing language skills is one of the core symptoms of autism, and differences or deficits in communication are seen in almost all individuals with ASDs. By middle childhood, up to half of children with autism have not developed functional speech. Early intervention with these children in teaching language or the use of augmentative and alternative communication interventions is imperative. Research shows that children who speak by the age of five or six years have the best outcome (Kasari, Paparella, Freeman, & Jahromi, 2008).

With higher functioning children, the pattern of speech development is typically more like Grace's experience—not much speech and then a torrent of verbiage that never seems to stop. What we have to remember (and share with school personnel) is that the social aspects of speech are frequently missing for children with high functioning ASDs, and this missing piece has far-reaching ramifications. Pragmatic language is what makes us able to have conversations with other people. It's taking turns, knowing when to start talking, and knowing when to stop talking. It's knowing which questions are okay to ask and when not to comment on something.

The hardest part of teaching pragmatic language skills is keeping up with the times. When I meet a child (usually a boy) with Asperger's disorder, I can almost always tell if he's had training in social skills and pragmatics. He walks up to me, makes a conscious effort to look me in the eye, sticks out his hand to shake, and says something like, "My name is Jason and I'm pleased to meet you." Very appropriate for meeting the queen or a job interview but not so much for making friends in high school. The proper greeting depends on the situation and, unlike other children, children on the spectrum do not know when to say "Yo, how's it hangin'" or any other greeting because they are not paying attention to what's going on around them. When they come to my office for the first time, they normally look at the ground, over my head, or right through me and mumble something. If their parents push, they may mumble a little louder.

Teaching your child social skills and pragmatic language is important, but you may not be the best person to do it. When we run social skills groups, my graduate students are much better at teaching the real lingo for greeting peers than I am because they are closer to the same social scene. I have also found that mixed groups (children with ASDs and normally developing children) are better than a group made up of only children on the spectrum. Be careful about the language your child picks up from TV or movies, too, as it's not always appropriate for all situations. There are some great books for teaching pragmatics and social skills. See the references below.

REFERENCES:

Baker, J. (2005). *Preparing for life. The complete guide for transitioning to adulthood for those with autism and Asperger's syndrome.* Arlington, TX: Future Horizons.

Baker, J. E. (2003). *Social skills training for children and adolescents with Asperger's syndrome and social-communication problems.* Arlington, TX: Future Horizons.

Kasari, C., Paparella, T., Freeman, S., & Jahromi, L. B. (2008). Language outcome in autism: Randomized comparison of joint attention and play interventions. *Journal of Consulting and Clinical Psychology, 76*(1), 125–137.

McAfee, J. (2002). *Navigating the social world. A curriculum for individuals with Asperger's syndrome, high functioning autism, and related disorders.* Arlington, TX: Future Horizons.

CHAPTER SEVEN

My, What a High Pain Tolerance You Have ... and What Sensitive Ears

One of the many things that I learned by reading the work of Dr. Temple Grandin is that the world is assaulting my kid's senses. This helps me to respond with compassion and accommodation to many behaviors that I would have previously treated as obnoxious. I can't stress this enough—my daughter's sensory issues are more of a challenge for her than they are for me.

Another terrific resource is *The Out-of-Sync Child* by Carol Kranowitz. Sometimes, when I am totally out of patience with some inexplicable behavior, I ask myself, "What would I do if I could feel the earth spinning under my feet?" Kids with Asperger's are considered to lack empathy. In fact, I often have to remind myself that I need to be empathic towards my kid as she encounters a world in which the volume is turned up too loud (and so are the colors) and she often needs to take a break from the extreme stimulation of simply being with other people.

The More It Changes,
the More It Stays the Same

Grace's pain tolerance fluctuates from nonexistent to something approaching normal. When she was younger, she literally didn't feel pain most of the time. We learned that pain is a very, very useful thing; it helps us to stop doing things that would otherwise be dangerous to us. Remember the light bulb and ant stories in Chapter One? Both of them could have turned really ugly. Fast-forward to age five. Grace extracted, over the course of a couple of weeks, four of her front teeth. I can say, with confidence that at least three of them were, at the most, only slightly loose. It involved blood on her fingers and face and she claimed that it didn't hurt. Each incident took her about half an hour. She would do it quietly in the back seat while we were on a car ride, or in bed after we'd turned out her light. She wouldn't make a sound until she excitedly announced what she'd done. It really freaked out her sisters. And me. And Ben.

I have to say that, although I am not a particularly squeamish person, this episode of Grace's totally freaked me out, too. I was afraid to let Bobbi know how much it bothered me, though.

At the same time, she was trashing a lot of stuff in the house. It was really gratuitous. Mercifully, such episodes come and go, and this one preceded some astonishing leaps in communication, reading, and hygiene. Sometimes it's important to remind ourselves that it isn't that intense all the time.

Every time we start to get a handle on the sensory stuff, it keeps changing. Referring to her son's pain tolerance, one mom reported:

It was very high until he was 3 and then it reversed. Now he screams at even a little pain.

— A., CALIFORNIA

Back to empathy for a moment. Our daughter had to be taught that others DO feel pain. This was actually a revelation to her. When you find something that is very aversive to your child (in Grace's case, one of the first things that we found was giving her a shower that was anything less than scalding hot, or, in her parlance, a *cold* shower). When your child is in the throes of responding to something he finds obnoxious, no matter how innocuous that thing might be to you, THAT'S the teachable moment. The light may turn on when you say, gently but firmly, "Honey, when you rip out handfuls of X's hair, she doesn't like it any better than you like feeling these labels on your clothes (or what have you)."

This Ain't Working the Way It's Supposed to Work

Sensory differences are very, very slippery. While my daughter's sensitive ears can barely stand entering a movie theater, she is willing to tolerate the pain if the movie is sufficiently interesting. I have actually watched in awe as her sensory sensitivities were trumped by her ability to hyperfocus on the action on the movie screen.

The first time I met Grace and her parents, the light bulb incident was still fresh in their minds—at least in the minds of Bobbi and Ben. Grace, it seemed, had no sense of pain and Bobbi had numerous stories to support that. Several months later, while playing with her sisters in my playroom, Grace ran headfirst into the door. She cried out in pain and fell to the floor. The adults (her parents and I) sat, open-mouthed, as Grace had a normal pain response. I admit it—I started to laugh with relief. Here was one less thing we had to worry about. Plus, the Sheahans haven't sued, yet.

Insensitivity to pain can be a serious problem. Children with ASDs are seven times more likely to engage in behavior that results in an injury to themselves (McDermott, Zhou, & Mann, 2008). McDermott and her colleagues examined hospital records for emergency treatment of injuries in children with ASDs and compared the rates to those of typically developing peers. They found children with ASDs were 20% more likely to have gone to the hospital for treatment of an injury. They had higher rates of treatment for poisoning (seven times the rate for the normally developing kids!); self-inflicted injury; and head, face, and neck injuries. The only group of injuries that was lower was sprains and strains. The authors hypothesized that this group of injuries was higher for normally developing children because they are more active in sports. Why do children with ASDs end up in hospital emergency rooms so often? McDermott et al. believe it is because they are less likely to perceive the risk of danger, are more impulsive, and are more likely to have repetitious behaviors that can be harmful. It makes sense to me. We must be vigilant with these children.

WHAT I WISH I'D KNOWN

I WISH I'D DISCOVERED CLOTHES
WITHOUT TAGS MUCH SOONER.

When she was two, my daughter adored the fireworks display. When she was three, she thought that she had been shot by a cannon and responded as if she had. Now, she's back to liking fireworks. Even though I now know that my child's senses are calibrated differently, they still don't work the way that I think they're supposed to work. While Grace adores my terrible singing and begs for lullabies, she went through years where she would cry and cover her ears at the singing in church. (Here's a funny aside: one of her siblings *actually complains about* my singing.) The different pitches, coming from so many different sources at once, are literally painful to Grace (say, as painful as my singing is to Mary). This, in concert with her other behavior, was really endearing to the other congregants, as one might imagine. At other times, she seemed to crave big noise.

For a common-sense explanation of sensory differences and a whole lot of ideas for activities that are both fun and good for your kid, I recommend to you two wonderful books: *1001 Great Ideas for Teaching and Raising Children with Autism Spectrum Disorders,* by Ellen Notbohm and Veronica Zysk and *The Autism Manual of Skills and Drills* by Elizabeth Scott and Lynne Gillis. These are books that you should own and keep within easy reach. In both of these books, the authors give terrific ideas for things to do for a child with sensory differences. A lot of them, like finger-painting, using chunky puzzles, and playing in the sandbox, were already popular at our house. Every time I read one of these books, I am emboldened to try something new. One morning, I let Grace and Mary "squeeze" the oatmeal after it got cold. I must admit, I expected more excitement from them. Also, a longer playtime. Mary was totally repulsed by the idea, and Grace loved it for about ten minutes and then got very insistent that we get them a bath going. The bath, in our house, can be a sensory escape involving sisters, bubbles, plastic toys, and (the kids' fave) ice cubes. I have heard many moms say that putting their kids in the tub cures many moods. My response to many problems is: "Put 'em in water."

WHAT I WISH I'D KNOWN

WHEN MY CHILD IS LAYING WASTE TO MY HOUSE, SOMETIMES
SHE'S NOT BEING NAUGHTY; SHE'S "SENSORY SEEKING."
FOR HER SAFETY AND FOR THE PRESERVATION OF MY HOUSE,
IT'S MY JOB TO FIND THE TEXTURE (OR WHAT HAVE YOU)
THAT SHE'S CRAVING. SQUEEZING OATMEAL, PETTING A
FABRIC SAMPLE, OR DANCING ON BUBBLE WRAP IS A LOT
LESS DAMAGING THAN DESTROYING THE COUCH.

You also have much more power to redirect than you may think. Instead of simply taking the magic marker away from your budding tattoo artist, you might say, "Oh! You need to scribble on something! Here is a piece of paper." Incidentally, we've banished permanent markers and oil-based paints to the greatest degree possible. Our kids can spend hours painting the swing set or "washing" the car.

If your child insists on writing on herself, you can have her lie down on a big piece of paper (we buy it by the roll) and trace her, then the two of you can color all over her image with crayons, markers, finger paint, or whatever. Some days, I just let her write all over herself and then take a long bubble bath. I have also been known to allow my kids to finger-paint the inside of the tub (and themselves) before turning the water on. I have whiled away many hours supervising bubble baths with a book or a laptop on my knees. How do you think I got this book written?

Daddy's Chin

You'll be amazed what sensory stuff your child will crave. My daughter Grace likes it when her daddy doesn't shave. She also loves for me to roll on her in my bed (yes, *roll on her*), which poses an interesting challenge: do I give her the sensory stimulation that she craves, or do I risk teaching her how to smoosh others? For a child who is challenged in the empathy department, and whose understanding of what is dangerous doesn't translate smoothly from one situation to another, this is a real challenge. I don't have an answer on this one. You just have to use your best judgment.

WHAT I WISH I'D KNOWN

SENSORY DIFFERENCES ARE OFTEN SOME OF THE FIRST CLUES THAT A CHILD HAS AN AUTISM SPECTRUM DISORDER. FOR US, THEY WERE OBVIOUS LONG BEFORE LANGUAGE DIFFICULTIES OR OTHER ISSUES CAME TO THE FORE. IT'S EMBARRASSING NOW TO THINK OF ALL OF THE TIMES THAT I THOUGHT, "MY LITTLE HUMAN CANNONBALL! I REALLY DO HAVE TO WATCH OUT FOR HER, DON'T I?" AND DIDN'T CLUE IN TO THE BIGGER PICTURE. NOW, WHEN I SEE A CHILD AT THE CIRCUS WHO IS COVERING HIS EARS AND GOING INTO THE FETAL POSITION, I DON'T THINK, "HE MUST BE TIRED," OR "WHAT A BADLY BEHAVED KID!" INSTEAD, I THINK, "THAT KID IS LITERALLY IN PAIN RIGHT NOW." IT'S ALSO GOOD TO REMEMBER THAT OTHERS MAY VIEW MY CHILD'S BEHAVIOR WITH A LESS SEASONED OR COMPASSIONATE EYE.

ALSO, I WISH I'D KNOWN NOT TO GIVE MY FOUR-YEAR-OLD THE "ICE PACK" FILLED WITH GEL GOO ON THE WAY HOME FROM THE ZOO.

Sensory differences are huge and confusing when we're talking about children with ASDs. Part of the confusion stems from the fact that sensory problems are not part of the diagnosis for autism—at least not now. That could change with the next edition of the diagnosis book. In the meantime, it's a pretty safe bet that your child has some type of sensory issue. Baker, Lane, Angley, and Young (2008) report that as many as 95% of children with ASDs have sensory processing difficulties. Sensory processing difficulties are exclusive of any sensory impairments such as blindness, deafness, etc. They occur in individuals whose sensory organs are intact and unimpaired.

Note: *Sensory issues are not limited to children on the spectrum. Lots of children have them—so do lots of adults. Try not to use a sensory issue to diagnose your neighbor's child.*

Dunn, Saiter, and Rinner (2002) report there are "seven basic sensory systems within the nervous system: sound, touch, vision, taste, smell, movement, and body position" (p. 173). The cerebral cortex and brainstem are responsible for managing information that comes in through the visual, auditory, vestibular (balance), and proprioceptive (body movement and position) systems (Baker et al.). These systems provide information from the surrounding environment, the individual's body, and the individual's interaction with the environment. Our brains make meaning out of all the information that is bombarding our sensory systems. In the case of children with ASDs, the problem comes when they try to use or process the information (Dunn et al.). When sensory information is integrated and processed effectively, children develop good adaptive skills, are able to learn, and have coordinated movements (Baker et al., p. 867). When it's not, all bets are off.

One of the most commonly used models of sensory processing (originally proposed by Dunn) looks at two concepts: neurological thresholds and self-regulation strategies. A neurological threshold is the amount of input required before the nervous system responds. "When a person has high thresholds, this means that it takes a lot of input for the nervous system to take notice and then generate a response" (Dunn et al., p.

173). If a child is focused on something else, such as a video game, their threshold is very high for your voice. It takes a while for them to hear you and then respond. Sometimes you have to unplug the game. "When a person has low thresholds, this means that it takes very little input for the nervous system to take notice, and lots of responses are generated" (p. 173). As Bobbi has pointed out, children with ASDs can have low thresholds for certain sounds and they generate responses to let you know that (i.e., covering their ears, screaming, crying, trying to get away, etc.).

Dunn et al. describe the self-regulation continuum as "the range of strategies a person might use in responding to task and environmental demands. A person who resorts to passive strategies has a tendency to let things happen; a person who uses active strategies reveals a tendency to generate responses to control input" (p. 173). There are four basic types of sensory processing and they are not mutually exclusive. As the mother in California reported, the type of sensory processing children use can change and we know that different environments or stimuli require different types of processing.

As I said, there are four basic types: low registration, sensation seeking, sensory sensitivity, and sensation avoiding. Children with low registration appear to be uninvolved in the world. They don't seem to hear what's going on around them and are the children most likely to be presumed deaf. Their hearing may seem to come and go and ear infections may be blamed. They are said to have "selective hearing." These children appear clumsy and need more information from their muscles and joints to get them going. Occupational therapists (OTs) may suggest having them wear weighted vests or ankle weights to make them more aware of their bodies. [Note: Despite the frequent use of weighted vests with children on the spectrum, I could not find any research to indicate that this practice is beneficial. See Stephenson and Carter (2009) for a review]

Children who are sensation or sensory seeking are very active and are hypothesized to be seeking additional sensory input from the environment. They are constantly moving around, and invade others' personal space during conversations. Some make repeated noises or babble to themselves because they enjoy the way the sounds feel (Dunn et al.). Some engage in inappropriate licking, smelling, or touching

(Baker et al.). One of the ten-year-old boys I see fits this pattern perfectly. He is constantly touching, smelling, and staring at things. He rocks in his chair, swings his arms around as he walks, and is constantly making noises. Originally diagnosed with Attention-Deficit/Hyperactivity Disorder (ADHD) as a young child, his mother discovered that working with an OT on his sensory issues has been very helpful. Now, when he's having a particularly difficult time, he stands on his head or does push-ups against a wall. This has helped at home but he is still struggling at school where other students have little tolerance for his behavior and teachers will not allow him to do the exercises.

Children with sensory sensitivity tend to be hyperactive and distractible. They notice more sensory stimuli and frequently complain about it. They use passive strategies and make comments rather than removing themselves from the situation (Dunn et al.). One boy I know spent an hour meeting with the counselor at school about a particularly nasty habit the boy had acquired. When I asked how the meeting went, he stated, "That man has a lot of nose hairs." He couldn't recall a thing the man said.

Sensation avoiding children have a repertoire of behaviors aimed at decreasing the amount of sensory stimuli coming in to them. They set up rules and routines with the express purpose of avoiding sensations. "Predictable patterns of behavior provide a high rate of familiar sensory input while simultaneously limiting the possibility of unfamiliar input" (Dunn et al., p. 176). For example, a child may refuse to participate in circle time in kindergarten because she knows she has a greater chance of being bumped by another child if she is sitting on the rug.

Children may use one type of processing for auditory stimuli and another type for visual stimuli. Many children with ASDs have difficulty processing auditory information. They may be overly sensitive to sounds or completely unresponsive to them. As a result, they appear uninvolved in the world around them. Visual processing is often a strength for children on the spectrum. They successfully complete difficult puzzles and recreate complicated patterns with blocks. Some children may stare intently at items, holding them close to their eyes. This leads parents to suspect vision problems but eye examinations seldom find a visual impairment. Siegel (1996) reports children in her experience tend to stare at objects that are long and straight, like twigs, or things that wiggle, like rubber bands.

Children with sensory processing difficulties frequently have more behavior problems and/or emotional problems. Pfeiffer, Kinnealey, Reed, and Herzberg (2005) found that children with Asperger's disorder and low sensory thresholds (i.e., sensory defensiveness) were more likely to suffer from anxiety. They found that sensory stimuli triggers a "fight or flight reaction" to stimuli that would not bother others. They hypothesize a relationship between anxiety and hypersensitivity and a corresponding relationship between depression and hyposensitivity to sensory stimuli (Pfeiffer et al.). Both anxiety and depression are frequently seen in individuals with Asperger's disorder. "The person becomes anxious due to constant overreaction to insignificant information in the environment … [and] depression is a defense reaction in order to cope with anxiety" (p. 336).

Children with sensory issues are most comfortable at home where the environment and the stimuli coming from it are familiar. School environments contain many new sights and sounds on a daily basis and can be stressful for children. Being stuck in a one-piece desk/chair makes movement difficult and the overloaded bulletin boards and art projects hanging from the ceilings of elementary classrooms are visually overwhelming. Walking down the halls during passing periods, especially in middle schools and high schools, is a sensory experience that I try to avoid. The same can be said for many activities in the community. While many children enjoy a trip to a crowded amusement park or zoo, it can be torturous for a child with sensory issues. The sights, sounds, smells, and constant bumping by strangers are more than enough to trigger a catastrophic reaction or meltdown. It is important to rethink outings and vacations. Trying to cram as much fun into a day as possible is not going to be fun for your child or for you. Be willing to take it slow, break it into pieces, and leave before the tantrum.

Sometimes we just have to respond to behavior without really knowing what to call it. I could spend the rest of my life trying to figure out whether certain behaviors fall into the "sensory differences" category, or whether I'm just seeing my daughter hyperfocus, or maybe she really is just blowing me off. Rather than try to rewrite the preceding sentence, let me just give you an example. I was in the car with the windows up and Ben was outside the car, out of my sight, trying to get my attention. When he came up to the door, I was startled and I jumped; he was frustrated and felt that I'd been blowing him off. I made both of us laugh by saying, "Well, now I know what it feels like to be Grace."

REFERENCES:

Baker, A. E., Lane, A., Angley, M. T., & Young, R. L. (2008). The relationship between sensory processing patterns and behavioural responses in autistic disorder: A pilot study. *Journal of Autism and Developmental Disorders, 38,* 867-875.

Dunn, W., Saiter, J., & Rinner, L. (2002). Asperger's syndrome and sensory processing: A conceptual model and guidance for intervention planning. *Focus on Autism and Other Developmental Disabilities, 17*(3), 172-185.

Kranowitz, C. S. (2005). *The out-of-sync child: Recognizing and coping with sensory processing disorder (rev.).* New York, NY: Perigee.

McDermott, S., Zhou, L., & Mann, J. (2008). Injury treatment among children with autism or pervasive developmental disorder. *Journal of Autism and Developmental Disorders, 38,* 626-633.

Notbohm, E., & Zysk, V. (2004). *1001 great ideas for teaching and raising children with autism spectrum disorders.* Arlington, TX: Future Horizons.

Pfeiffer, B., Kinnealey, M., Reed, C., & Herzberg, G. (2005). Sensory modulation and affective disorders in children and adolescents with Asperger's disorder. *American Journal of Occupational Therapy, 59*(3), 335-345.

Siegel, B. (1996). *The world of the autistic child. Understanding and treating autistic spectrum disorders.* New York, NY: Oxford Press.

Stephenson, J., & Carter, M. (2009). The use of weighted vests with children with autism spectrum disorders and other disabilities. *Journal of Autism and Developmental Disorders, 39,* 105-114.

CHAPTER EIGHT
What Can I Do about These Weird Behaviors?

Maybe Eye Contact Is Overrated

As we touched on earlier, the obvious, attention-getting behaviors may not be the most important ones to address. People will notice a child's lack of eye contact or social skills and try to get that child to "act normal." Such efforts are, in my humble opinion, both futile and beside the point. Behaviors that are odd (unusual speech patterns, lack of eye contact, hyper-focus, solitary play, bagel-related obsessions) are not front-burner issues when there are also behaviors that are dangerous (hurting oneself or others). Repetitive behaviors might drive you nuts, but in the grand scheme, they may not be the first priority. Grace loses it if someone sits in the wrong seat at the dinner table, which gets interesting when we have guests. While it's normal (well, normal for *us*) for her to have a response, we also let her know that she can leave the table before we are going to spend our meal as hostages to her tantrum. This is an area where Dr. DeOrnellas has had to train us so that we can train our child. It's so important, I'm gonna put a box around it:

> **We can prepare ourselves for immature responses without giving her the idea that such responses are acceptable.**

When Bobbi refers to the strange, attention-getting behaviors that may or may not take center stage, she is referring to those symptoms of autism with which most people are familiar—the "restricted repetitive and stereotyped patterns of behavior, interests, and activities" (DSM-IV-TR, 2000, p. 75). We briefly discussed each of those in Autism 101 but it is important to have a clear understanding of what each looks like.

The first is an overwhelming interest in something. Attwood (2003) estimates that 90% of individuals with Asperger's disorder have these interests. In my experience, boys with HFASDs tend to be interested in accumulating knowledge in a particular area. Some of the areas I have seen include Egyptology, Star Wars, military history, trains, skyscrapers, vacuum cleaners, washing machines, weather, and sports statistics. Girls with HFASDs also have special interests, such as dolls and clothing, but the interests of the fifteen or so girls I have worked with have focused more on collecting things than on accumulating facts. For example, I worked with a young teenager who has collected beads and sequins since she was very young. She has boxes and boxes of them. One girl collects pencils and I can count on her to sneak several pencils from my office during each visit. Another carries a bag of pencil sharpeners around with her at all times. She reportedly has hundreds of them she has collected since she was quite young. A young adult I know collects DVDs—she doesn't watch them, just keeps them in stacks in her room. Some girls are very interested in horses. I have had reams of paper brought to my office with horse bloodlines painstakingly written on them and hundreds of photos of horses that have been printed from the Internet. I also knew a young woman in her mid-thirties who collected snakes. Although these interests may change over time, most individuals maintain a level of interest in something that exceeds what most would consider normal.

Some children with HFASD have an interest in numbers or calculation and are able to work multiplication problems with four or five digits in their head. A little boy I knew in a preschool class repeatedly drew very accurate pictures of the electric transmission tower he could see from his classroom window. I have heard of individuals who could tell you the day of the week that a particular date fell upon hundreds of years ago.

There are problems that can result from having an obsession with a particular topic. Sometimes the topic is not a healthy one. For example, adolescents may have an interest in bomb-making or pornography. If your child appears headed in that direction, it is best to help them come up with a new topic of interest. For example, the bomb-making enthusiast can be rechanneled into physics (as one ten-year-old I know has done) or military history. In the case of pornography, counseling and straight talk about sex appears warranted.

The most common problem I run into is the individual's need to talk about their topic. This need is like a compulsion and when the need is not met, the individual with ASD can become frustrated and angry. This causes problems at home and at school. It is extremely boring and frustrating for others to listen to hours of talk about how many soldiers on each side died at Gettysburg. The individual with ASD knows way more about this topic than most of us ever wanted to know and they do not read the social cues we are giving off. These social cues include looking away, glazed over eyes, turning away, running away, etc. I have seen a boy continue on and on about Egyptology to an empty lunch table. All of the other students had moved away and he was oblivious. When I work with children who have this problem, I teach them a number of tricks for knowing when to stop talking and let someone else talk and I teach them how to read those social cues. This can be done individually or in a small group.

Note: *Although it would seem to make sense that you could pair a boy fascinated with Star Wars with another boy fascinated with Star Wars for play dates and friendships, I have not found it to work very well. Both boys want to talk and neither wants to listen. Each considers himself the expert on the topic. I have found it goes better when we pair boys with different interests and teach them the give and take of conversation. They are each more comfortable with their own topic and don't have the anxiety that someone might know more than they do.*

Our challenge as parents and professionals is to "transform the 'special interest' into a functional, useful activity or learning activity" (Siegel, 1996, p. 69). For example, one of the adults I worked with was always interested in (obsessed with) trains as a child. As an adult, he is not able to work for a railroad but he volunteers in an amusement park and drives children around a track on a small train on weekends. As the engineer, he thoroughly enjoys himself and it seems to meet his need for being with trains. When I asked how he liked working with children, however, he seemed surprised. I think he loses himself in the activity and the children are just part of the scenery. Currently, I'm working with a young man who has an incredible knowledge of baseball. We're looking into jobs with the local baseball team. One of my "horse girls" is working at a stable after school. If you have any ideas about the Star Wars or pencil sharpener obsessed, let me know.

Put That Down and Look at Me!

Entire books have been written about autistic obsessions. Our kids pick a topic and they do not let it go. Personally, I would get bored watching the same video OVER and OVER again. My child does not share this view. I have come to understand and accept this. This understanding and acceptance has also influenced my choice of the videos that I'll allow in my house. Whether I am screening for content (aggression, language, etc.) or simply my knowledge that I'd rather have a sharp stick in my eye than see/hear a particular character or song *ad nauseum*, I view new acquisitions to our video library with the eagle eye of a critic. I must also add that

Asperger's has made me more careful than most about resisting the temptation to allow my child to watch TV all day long. Conversely, I have also baffled some of my friends by allowing Grace to take "video breaks" when other children are around. While my friends may think that this is lazy parenting on my part, my guess is that they'd prefer a half-hour of movie time to having Grace spin until she crashes into their child.

The Dinosaur Doesn't Fall Far from the Tree

To the extent that you share your child's interest (or can steer him towards something that doesn't send you screaming into the night), it can be an opportunity to build your relationship with him. Yes, this sounds obvious, but it is tempting to see only the behavior and miss the child. For example, Grace is very interested in cooking. She loves to stir, pour, and generally make a mess. When I'm not cleaning up messes (or yelling at her for making a mess), I use this as an opportunity to affirm her. When you consider that whatever your child is doing at that moment is The Most Important Activity in the History of the World, it follows naturally that it is music to her ears to hear, "Mommy loves to bake too!" "You're a good cook." "Wow, can you help me stir this?"

Mary's godmother, Genifer, is especially good at integrating her kids into what she is doing. When they closed on their house, she brought the (preschool-aged) kids. How, you may reasonably ask, did she pull this off? She got them their own little stampers and paper and prepared them beforehand. While Mom and Dad were signing and the notary was stamping away, so were they! They will always remember the day that they helped to buy their house, and now it is a shared memory.

When our kids have differences and limitations, it's easy to forget that they really do want to join in what we're doing. I also do believe that they get the message when we think they're weird. This is devastating to any child. Often, I'll catch myself in the middle of wondering why Grace is doing the same farm puzzle over and over and over and instead of fussing or telling her she's wasting her time, I'll say something like, "Oh, honey, you love that puzzle because you love Daddy and he grew up on a farm!" or "Wow, you're getting really good at that."

Easier said than done, but practice will make perfect. Won't it? (Somebody please tell me it will. I'm a little obsessed.)

Your kid may obsess about stuff that's basically harmless, but just, well, weird.

> *Once he noticed I like my bagels put in the toaster twice, that's how he wants it. It doesn't matter if I dial up the toaster so it toasts for a longer time: he still gets upset that it wasn't "down twice."*
>
> — J., Massachusetts

It sounds obvious when you write it down, but wanting your child to communicate and to appear normal can be a powerful urge. Safety really is a higher priority. Also, keep in mind that when you think that you're working on one thing (i.e., potty training), your kid's brain figures out something else (e.g., aggression). The reality is, my daughter's brain is wired differently than mine. Sometimes I think I'm working on one thing (eye contact or potty training) and I see a burst of progress in another area (say, communication or aggression). In our case, we also don't work on more than one thing at a time—even if "at a time" goes on for a month. When Grace is engaged with reading, she isn't thinking about math. I could panic about math, but I know from experience that she will soon exclusively focus on math, possibly for weeks or months.

It's good to know that all I can do is roll with it and keep doing what works. It's also good to know that some things really do resolve themselves with the passage of time. Dr. DeOrnellas has trained me to ask a few questions before I'm allowed to freak out:

1. Would I really worry about this behavior if she were half her chronological age? If not, then there's a good chance that it's just a developmental delay and she'll grow out of it.

2. Would I worry about this behavior if she were a boy? (My apologies to boys; I'm just sayin.')

If the answer to either question is no, then maybe I need to switch to decaf and find something better to worry about.

Sometimes the answer to both of these questions is yes. Then, I ask myself, Am I sure I haven't seen this behavior before? Sometimes it's easy to get caught up in the moment and forget that yes, she stopped spinning last time when I caught her in my arms and tickled her, or that I had to take her face in my hands and say, "Listen to me with your face" to get her attention.

All of this has also been a crash course in good problem-solving; start with what works. When that doesn't work, shift strategies when necessary and try, try again. We will discuss specific strategies—lots of them—but attitude is more important than the specifics. You will figure out what works, and when it stops working, you will figure out something else. Start believing this, and your world will change.

We found that we overreacted to new problems at first, and then quickly realized that overreacting is a full-time job. Now, we try to limit our overreactions to safety issues, which wind up taking priority over communication issues. Thus, the long-term struggle to get my daughter to use her words and to look at us gets treated like a chronic condition and is, sometimes, on the back burner, while other things that crop up demand our immediate (and often undivided) attention for a period of time. This may sound funny, but that cycle begins to take on a rhythm that is almost comforting. Almost. It is also helpful to keep a journal. There are weeks, and sometimes months, that are so trying that you may be tempted to give up. A journal will give you something to look back upon and see how far you've come; it will also remind you that the really tough cycles really do come and go. Just this past year, we realized that our daughter seems to consistently have difficulties at the same time each year. I could speculate about several possible causes, but suffice it to say that this year, we plan to be prepared for the Annual Fall Meltdown.

"She's Just Shy"

I am on a constant learning curve when it comes to my daughter's need to be in familiar places and/or in small, manageable groups and/or to keep outings short. For me, it was critical to learn the Early Warning Signs and head off the meltdowns.

I am now willing to look like an overprotective (okay, crazy) mom, even when it means I have to quickly hustle my kids out of the park, the dental office, or what have you. (You may not recognize the early stages of what I call the Launch Sequence, but just thank me and get out of my way as I rush with my kids towards the exit.)

Every child is going to be different, but if I start to leave when Grace gets that look in her eye, then I don't have to worry about what she's going to do in the parking lot. If I wait until she's started to get increasingly uncooperative or expansive with her movements (or to shrink into a corner), I've waited too long. Once my child starts the Launch Sequence, all bets are off. When she gets to a certain level of agitation, it is going to take her a couple of days to regain control of her emotions and her bodily functions (yes, you read that right), and she will need a lot of holding and a lot of downtime.

I recently re-read *The Curious Incident of the Dog in the Night-Time,* and I found myself nodding my head at the (fictional) autistic narrator's description of how he felt barraged by unfamiliar signs in a subway station, as if the words and the colors were shouting at him (Mark Haddon, Random House 2003). This is so important to understand, and I'll say it again: our kids aren't trying to annoy us. They really do feel barraged by the sights, sounds, and people that seem totally normal to us. Sometimes there is just too much to look at; other times, too many senses are engaged at once.

My solution? I try to err on the side of underwhelming her, even if it means that we miss the birthday party (or just come for the second half of it). If I have a choice between showing her a video or letting her listen to a story on CD, the CD is better for her because it only involves one of her senses. I have learned to deflect the well-meaning (and fearless) friends who say, "Oh, go ahead and bring all of your kids!" While *they* may be able to handle our differences with aplomb—and God bless 'em, I say—I can't put my child in situations that I know are going to freak her out. This is a tough concept for others to get; it's not just that I don't want my child sneaking off to break her breakables, eat sugar by the handful, or whack her kid with a rock. It's also that I now understand that Grace experiences sensory overload like having rusty nails run over her skin while flashing a bright light in her face. I actually struggled with the temptation to add annoying graphics, strobe lights, showers of confetti (let's make that confetti to which you have an allergic reaction), and sound effects to make the point, but I think that you get it. We also remind Grace, when we are *en route* to a birthday party, that it is okay if it is too crowded or busy for her, and if she asks us to take her out for a break or to take her home, we respond immediately. You may have this discussion with your child a hundred times or more before he finally makes this request, but you are offering him an important skill—leaving of his own volition when he is *starting* to feel overwhelmed—that he can use for his entire life.

At a recent birthday party, Grace seated herself at the edge of an active group engaged in a circle game and went into the fetal position with a pillow over her head. I asked her (a couple of times) if she wanted me to remove her, and she assured me that she was having a ball. The other kids, who know her well, were totally unfazed, and Grace told me several times afterwards what a great time she'd had. In reflecting upon it, I was really proud that her behavior—which looked more stereotypically "autistic" than usual—really was a successful way for her to manage the situation.

Leave 'Em Wanting More

As a general rule, the key to being a good guest is knowing when to leave. When Grace was smaller, she couldn't handle much more than half an hour of sensory overload, which could mean the mall, a party, or just being at someone's house with people moving and talking and playing. Now, that time has more than doubled, but we also build in a lot of safety valves. We often arrive late and we try to leave *before* the meltdown starts.

Accommodations include everything from modifications to our house to how we spend our time. Half of a party is a victory, not a defeat. We don't try to do two things in a day, nor do we do big, interesting things two days in a row. If we are at the park, I am going to be pushing her on the swing for a good bit of that time. If we are at someone's house, I might take her to a quiet room and just hold her for a few minutes. Sometimes, we can go to a birthday party or park and plan to leave early; other times, we take two cars so that our other kids can stay with one parent while the other parent takes Grace home. While sitting and focusing at library storytime is just peachy for my child (all of them, actually), and an hour at the park with a bunch of kids can work, two hours at the park and a couple of chocolate cupcakes is a recipe for disaster: a messy, embarrassing, public disaster that involved seeing those cupcakes again. (I'll just take this opportunity to say that the manager of the CVS at the corner of 78 and 544 in Wylie, Texas deserves to be publicly honored for her kind-heartedness, especially in light of the mess she had to clean up.)

Here is another example from my own life. I wanted to kick myself. I was sure that I had checked the schedule and that the soccer class was going to be held outdoors, not in the gym. Although she can tolerate it on a good day, I usually don't even try to take Grace into the gym, what with the acoustics and the proximity of other human bodies—moving human bodies who dare to think that they can touch her soccer ball. I was so sure that I'd checked out everything. In addition to confirming that Grace was at the top of the age range for the class, and that the class was short (four brief half-hour sessions), small (six kids max), and (I thought) outdoors, I had prevailed upon Grace to bring her *sister's* soccer ball and to discuss with her repeatedly the fact that the other kids might touch her or the ball and that was okay, it was part of the game. Given the fact that it wasn't her own soccer ball, she accepted this.

None of the foregoing prevented her from attempting to return to the womb when we walked into the gym. Yep, it had been moved indoors.

The coach reasonably attempted to draw her out. He encouraged her to join the group. "She's just shy," I mumbled apologetically as we beat a hasty retreat. Two hours later, Grace continued to plead with me to confirm that she wouldn't have to go to soccer again. Any soccer. Ever. In any place. At any time. When I asked her how she felt about going to soccer or why she didn't like it, she just said, "I felt shy." I'm fairly sure that she'd never heard the word "shy" before that day. When I asked her what she meant by "shy," I couldn't tease an answer out of her. I already knew that she wouldn't have the words for how she felt. Giving her those words, and keeping her out of loud, unfamiliar spaces, are part of *my* job. As of this writing, the soccer incident was nearly two years ago, and she hasn't touched a soccer ball since. She still balks at the entrance of a basketball gym and refuses to go in.

This is a good time to bring up the topic of activities designed for kids with special needs. If you are in doubt about whether your child may benefit from an activity designed specially for children with special needs—say, art class, dance class, or a sport—I want to strongly encourage you to err on the side of trying. If it's not a fit, you will know right away, but, then again, you and your child may just have one of the most pleasant surprises of your life, both in terms of your child's response to the activity and the wonderful, supportive people you will meet. The smaller groups and enthusiastic helpers were just the ticket for our family. We will talk lots more about this in Chapter 11.

We have also found that the "smaller is better" principle works for spectator-type activities. For example, we learned the hard way that a small, regional circus in an outdoor tent with a single elephant is okay, and that a large, fancy circus with a dozen elephants isn't going to work, at least for now. In the smaller setting, my daughter bravely rode the elephant while I sat paralyzed with fear behind her. In the larger, louder setting, we cut our losses by leaving at the intermission.

WHAT I WISH I'D KNOWN

THAT GRACE IS MUCH, MUCH BRAVER THAN I AM. ESPECIALLY WHEN IT COMES TO ELEPHANTS.

The next behavior is a *strict observance of routines*. While a few individuals with HFASD are able to provide their own structure to the world, most have considerable difficulty organizing the world on their own and need others to provide it for them. However, once a routine has been established, it must be observed. This can be problematic in a number of ways. When others don't know the routine and inadvertently do things differently, children can become very upset. Some situations that change the routine are outside the control of caregivers. These include fire drills, construction on the road that requires a deviation in the trip to school, or running out of something that is required for the routine or ritual. One boy I know was devastated when the grocery store stopped carrying the brand of cereal that he ate every morning. These changes in the routine or unscheduled events are very uncomfortable and children may appear disoriented or spend hours talking about the change. When you know ahead of time that there is going to be any sort of change, it is best to create a Social Story and start preparing your child. If they use a picture schedule, be sure to go over the changes and let them help you rearrange the schedule.

Having a Routine without Feeling Like a Hostage

Our children need routine much more than other kids do. This is one of those lessons that you continue to learn and re-learn, and it's supposed to get easier. For example, a change from one bed to another, or the loss of a comfort item may trigger a tantrum, a regression, or a fortnight without sleep. We had to get it through our heads that our child, who seems so very, very even-keel, experiences these disruptions the way that we would experience the death of a loved one. Any change that is predictable can—and should—be preceded by a great deal of preparation. I'm talking repetitive preparation.

Let me give an example of what I'm talking about. When Grace was four, her sister had a contagious illness, and we moved Grace out of their shared room for a few days. It took her three weeks to stop crying and melting down. (There were other kinds of fallout, but I'll spare you now and refer you to Chapter Five.) Even though I moved her entire bed, all of her things, and even her decorations, she experienced this change like a hurricane evacuee. She insisted on moving back as soon as she could, but then she grieved over that change as well.

Oddly enough, we are quite able to travel with Grace; she frequently asks to stay at a hotel because—you guessed it—the rooms are all the same.

This is an area in which our needs are different from our kids' needs. I mean, really, really different. While we would suffer from lack of friends, our kids can go for miles without a friend in sight, but don't mess with their bottle cap collections (or what have you). If you haven't read *Mozart and the Whale* by Jerry and Mary Newport (or seen the movie version), you should. Jerry's description of Mary's attempt to tidy up some of his things makes this point very well. His response was, shall we say, extreme.

He absolutely cannot function without routine. We do the same things usually every day. Sometimes we change things just a bit to help him learn to adjust. Life isn't going to adjust for him so we have to try to help him adjust. He does ok as long as we don't try to change too many things all at once.

Whenever we did anything out of the ordinary like stay at someone's house, he would cry for days.

— J., Ohio

WHAT I WISH I'D KNOWN

WHEN A CHILD TAKES OFF ALL OF HIS CLOTHES
AND HIDES AT THE SUGGESTION THAT YOU ATTEND
A FUNCTION, YOU PROBABLY WANT TO SKIP IT—
EVEN IF IT'S A SPECIAL FUNCTION FOR SPECIAL NEEDS KIDS.
IT'S NOT GOING TO GO WELL.

Who's in Charge Here?

Let's talk about routines; our kids are really big on them. To tell you the truth, this was a difficult section for me to write. Not because it was painful or that I had nothing to say, but I found the empty computer screen just staring at me every time I'd try to attack the subject. One day, as I was driving down the road, the reason for my difficulty came to me. (Prepare for another of Bobbi's Duh! moments.) I don't have a lot of brilliant ideas about Grace's routine because it's not mine; *it's hers.* I didn't really come up with it; she did. I have, at different times, tried a picture schedule and creative uses of the kitchen timer, but I finally wised up and realized that any routine I impose on Grace is only going to cause frustration. She finds comfort in her routine and she needs it. *It's hers.* Most of the time, our life has a nice rhythm and we do a lot of the same things each day, or each week on the same day. It works for all of us. Yes, we have collaborated to create our life, but she is very, very good at letting us know what isn't working. She likes repetition a lot more than most kids her age. I have never, ever heard her say that she is tired of her favorite foods, which comprise a very short list. She likes to play with the same toys all the time, and she will notice minor changes in our home. By "notice," I mean that she may scream, flip out, and/or lose control of some bodily functions in the wake of an unexpected change in the orientation of the couch or the kitchen table.

DR. DeORNELLAS SAYS

YOU CAN'T SET THE ROUTINE;
YOU JUST HAVE TO RESPECT THE ROUTINE.

One of the ways that I use this to my advantage is to make slight variations on themes that she likes. For example, she likes it when I tell the story of a princess who only likes the color red. When I tell the story, I let her name the characters and fill in a lot of the details. It's a good way to get her engaged and talking, and we both like the predictability of the story. In addition to the fact that I frequently change the color that the princess likes, I use this story to introduce new vocabulary words, or I can tailor the story to what I know is coming up later in the day. "And then the princess went to the PARK where everything was…" and she'll say "Red!" and so on. When I am doing this, I have to carefully notice if my changes are upsetting her. Actually, it doesn't take a rocket scientist. She will melt down, cry, yell, and reprimand me in any way that she can (including physically) if she is displeased with how much I'm changing "her" story.

While we're on the topic of teaching by repetition, let me do a little repetition with you. This is something that Dr. DeOrnellas has been trying to teach us for a long time: the fact that Grace is wired differently doesn't mean that we should lower our standards for her behavior. While it's true that she may have an extreme emotional response to something that I say or do, I don't have to allow her to split my eardrums—or my lip—over it. One of the things that our kids really, really need from us is training in gentleness. I am going to say this in caps: YOU DO NOT HAVE TO ALLOW YOUR CHILD TO TRASH YOUR HOUSE, SPLIT YOUR EARDRUMS, OR BEAT YOU UP. It is going to take a lot more training for our kids than it is for other kids, but we must not proceed as if this kind of behavior is acceptable. They do not instinctively understand how their shrieking may impact others, no matter how sensitive their own hearing is. They may not want to be touched, but they have to be taught that they may not whack other people.

It is both comforting and hard to realize that my child, who doesn't mean anyone any harm, can lash out in response to stress and bite the dentist or knock a kid off a swing and truly lack insight into what she is doing. This is where I have to be her conscience as well as her voice. At some point, with enough repetition, the desired behaviors do become routine, even if they aren't really ever going to be instinctive.

The responses you teach your child should be responses you are willing to see/hear over and over again. For example, Grace learned how to apologize from *Anne of Green Gables*. If you didn't know better, you'd just think that she had really, really good manners.

"But I Don't Have My Bear with Me!"

Sometimes I have to remind myself that her mind and emotions are wired a little differently than mine. Once, when Grace was four, she burst into tears on the way to playgroup because she didn't have her teddy bear with her. Although we had been going to this playgroup on and off for months, she suddenly remembered that everyone had brought their bears to the first meeting as an ice-breaker, and she suddenly couldn't imagine walking in without it. Understanding why this meltdown happened helped me to respond with compassion and not annoyance. As a friend once said to me, "If my daughter vomited on me because she was undergoing chemotherapy, would I punish her for that? Of course not."

Many children with ASDs engage in stereotypical motor movements (i.e., stereotypies). They are more common, or perhaps more obvious, in lower functioning children but can be observed in higher functioning children as well. The most common are hand flapping, finger flicking, walking on tiptoe, rocking, grimacing, and pacing. Parents may not notice the motor movements because they attribute a purpose to them (Myles & Southwick, 1999). For example, when their child walks on his toes, they explain the behavior by saying he is pretending to be an animal. Doctors, teachers, and parents with more experience may be the first to tell the parent that there is a problem. Older children and adolescents may develop less obvious stereotypies such as rubbing their fingers together or flexing their fingers. Pacing during a stressful situation is common in adolescents and adults.

As a psychologist who conducts diagnostic evaluations of individuals with ASDs, I am privy to the whole range of stereotypies. Testing situations can be very stressful because it is frequently the first time they have been to my office and I am asking them to do things outside their comfort zone. When I mention them to parents, they sometimes seem surprised.

The purpose for stereotypical behaviors has been hypothesized. Myles and Southwick (1999) suggest they are a sort of overflow of behavioral response to the environment. The child is overwhelmed by sensory overload or stress and the behaviors "leak out." In this case, I have found that the individual is unaware of the behavior. When I ask a young man to stop pacing or a child to stop rocking, they frequently seem surprised to find themselves doing so. In some instances, the motor movements can become self-stimulating. The child gets lost in a motor movement that helps him to distance himself from an overwhelming environment. Parents should not allow the child to spend much time in self-stimulating or "stimming" behaviors, because they prohibit the child from participating in other activities that are important to their development. A recent study by Chen, Rodgers, and McConachie (2009) confirmed previous research that found a connection between the degree of sensory problems reported by mothers and the number of restricted and repetitive behaviors engaged in by their children with ASD.

Grace doesn't seem to have any obvious stereotypies, but she does share a family trait (I won't say which side, but it isn't my side) of picking at her fingernails in a very distinctive way. I have actually seen one of her infant cousins doing this in the crib. Her sister once was photographed engaging in this unique type of self-manicure while on a stage in front of an audience. As you will see from Dr. DeOrnellas' next section, this may also fall into another category.

Finally, there is a preoccupation with parts of objects. Children may be fascinated with spinning wheels on toy cars, strings on their clothing, their shoelaces, etc. With adolescents, I see a preoccupation with biting their fingernails or their cuticles. I've been in sessions with boys who could not focus on anything but a speck of mud on their shoes, pulling their socks up so that they are perfectly even, or tying their shoelaces so that both loops are the same length.

With individuals with HFASD, I find giving them something to hold in their hands (like a stress ball) helps to refocus their attention. I frequently try to talk teachers into trying this. Otherwise, we have students spinning coins or pencils on the tops of their desks or trying to squint through straws, or whatever else fascinates them at the moment. Unfortunately, I meet with resistance about half the time. Teachers worry that it will be distracting to other students. Sometimes there's the discussion of how it's not fair to give Johnny a stress ball if no one else in the class has a stress ball. Of course, it doesn't seem fair that Johnny has an ASD and the other students don't have one. (Can you tell this is a pet peeve of mine?) Other teachers, however, are open to trying new things and understand the real concept of fairness—that it's not about what's fair but about giving all students what they need to succeed. In the meantime, I'm working with Johnny to make sure he's not making a nuisance of the stress ball. When he does, there are consequences that he has known about all along and they are swiftly enforced.

There are a few other quirky behaviors we see in children with ASDs and this seems a good place to mention them. The first is lining things up. Bobbi describes this activity at her house.

Lining Up the Dolls

I have an illustration of how things can seem normal to us and escape our notice altogether. It also illustrates how Lucy is smarter than I am. I walked in on Grace recently as she was lining up all of the dolls in the dollhouse. Some days, she seriously wouldn't care if we had no other toys. For years now, I've thought, "I didn't suspect autism for the longest time because she was affectionate and didn't line up her toys." Of course, I may have been paying more attention to my child than the toys and just missing it, or maybe this is new behavior. I tend to think it's been happening under my nose, because apparently her sister Lucy had noticed this some time ago. While every case is unique and Grace is extra-normal in that regard, Lucy has been complaining for years about how "Grace messes up my set-ups" when they play with the dollhouse and all of the many small pieces that go with it. Lucy has even (fruitlessly) appealed to me to lock Grace out of the playroom when she (Lucy) is compelled to do a chore or do schoolwork or something else outside the playroom. I just chalked it up to little-kid possessiveness. What I now realize is that Grace was lining up the dolls and furniture—taking them out of the dollhouse and just lining them up—and that it was driving Lucy nuts!!

This is another one of those strange behaviors associated with ASDs. We see it in lower functioning children all the time but it is not often as apparent in the higher functioning children. I believe the lining up of objects is just one more way of ordering the universe for children with ASDs. We see the same behavior in ourselves when we have to straighten our desks before and after a big project. Unless your child is engaging in this activity to the exclusion of most everything else, I would say this is one of those things you should choose not to spend a lot of energy on. Sorry, Lucy.

LUCY SAYS

CAN'T I HAVE MY OWN PLAYROOM?
HOW ABOUT MY OWN DOLLHOUSE?

Another strange (in my opinion—although some parents take great pride in this skill) behavior or talent is the incredible rote memory that some children with ASDs have. It frequently starts at a very young age. Children with ASDs have an uncanny knack for hearing and repeating snippets of conversations. One of the very first autism assessments I conducted while working in the schools was of a three-year-old boy. For the entire assessment, he repeated dialog from television commercials. In Grace's case, refer back to her version of an apology earlier in this chapter.

Other children with ASDs learn information from their parents or siblings (I can't imagine where else they would get it) and replay it over and over as performance art. For example, one of the boys in our research study has been able to name all of the states and their capitals from the age of three. His mother related the story that he would do this for dinner guests. If he was sent to bed before finishing, he could always say which ones were left to say, even though he did not say them in any particular order. The Internet has many videos of very young children showing off their rote memories. One I have seen is of a very small child reciting capitals of all the countries in the world. He names countries I never even heard of and his proud parent can be seen following along with a list.

I don't want to sound grumpy about this and I truly understand the need for parents to find their children's talents. However, there is a downside to this talent. Children with this gift appear to know more than they do and expectations for them can be very high. Teachers and parents believe the child understands the concepts and become frustrated when they cannot perform a task using the concepts. For example, a child can recite all the steps for doing a math equation but be unable to work the problem.

Another problem is that "educators assume that good rote memory means that students can remember, at any time, pieces of information or events" (Myles & Southwick, 1999, p. 7). Unfortunately, individuals with ASDs store information differently in their brains and it can be difficult to retrieve on command. For example, if a student is asked to describe what happened to the "main character" he may have trouble finding the answer because he has stored that information under the main character's name, "John Jones." There may not be a link between "main character" and "John Jones" and the student cannot come up with the answer (Myles & Southwick).

Another thing we hear about, especially with individuals with Asperger's disorder, is theory of mind. Although it is still somewhat controversial, theory of mind is considered a sort of dividing line between those with Asperger's disorder and those with high-functioning autism. As we have previously discussed, trying to differentiate between the two disorders is controversial but it is important for parents and educators to understand the implications of theory of mind. Individuals who have difficulty with theory of mind find it hard to understand the emotions and thought processes of others. This is particularly true in social situations and I believe the added sensory stimulation of a social situation compounds the problem.

Myles and Southwick (1999) did a nice job of breaking down theory of mind into a problem list and I will borrow from them. If your son has problems with theory of mind, he is likely to have the following difficulties.

- First, he has a hard time explaining his own behaviors. "Why" questions are not effective and can be very frustrating. I find "what" and "how" questions work much better.

- Second, he probably doesn't really understand emotions—his own or anyone else's. He especially doesn't understand the subtleties of emotions. He does not understand that some situations are sort of sad or happy and other situations are extremely sad or happy. I find using a "feelings thermometer"—one for each feeling (happy, sad, mad, scared)—works well. We label the thermometer with different degrees of feelings and examples of when he felt that way.

- Third, your son has a hard time predicting how others are going to feel or respond. He probably doesn't understand that when you have a headache you will not be as receptive to his jokes or as forgiving of his bad behavior.

- Fourth, he has a hard time seeing things from someone else's perspective. Telling him to think about how his harsh words made someone feel will not work very well.

- Fifth, your son has trouble figuring out the intentions of others. This can leave him in the starring role as "butt of the joke" if he comes into contact with cruel or thoughtless (you can pretty much substitute "normal" here) children. Your son takes things literally and, unless he is taught, will not understand figures of speech, idioms, or plays on words. Most jokes soar over his head and, although he loves telling jokes, the ones he tells don't make sense. If your son really wants to tell jokes, get him a joke book and help him practice his delivery.

- Sixth, your son does not understand that his behavior impacts others. If he hits his sister and she doesn't want to play with him, he will not understand that it's because he hit her.

- Seventh, your son has difficulty taking turns in conversations, being polite, and making appropriate eye contact. This is especially true when he is talking about his favorite topic but is pervasive in most social interactions.

- Finally, your son may have difficulty separating fact from fiction. I find this to be especially true for those who are interested in science fiction. Star Wars, Pokémon, and the Mario Brothers are very real to some children (Myles & Southwick).

Lest you give up hope, Bobbi describes a recent conversation with Grace that shows she is beginning to develop words for her emotions.

You'll Never Know If You Don't Ask

I've learned not to be afraid to ask my child about some of the inexplicable things she's done. Suppressing my fear that I might tempt her to try it again, I asked Grace for details about the light-bulb-munching incident. Although years had passed since this event, her memory of it was quite clear. She surprised me by telling me that she had jumped from the bed and not the bookshelf (lending further credence to my belief that she can fly), and she told me that she did not swallow any glass because she started to swallow a little and it hurt her throat ("it felt like bees"), and that she spat it out. She also surprised me when she told me that the cuts she sustained on her hands had been painful. At the time, she was giving every indication of feeling no pain.

I could really relate to the following from R. in Illinois:

I wish my son could explain where all the negative thoughts that come out during an outburst come from. Are they things that others have told him or just things he thinks of but never talks about, just lets them out during an outburst.

Learning to experience and express emotions is harder for my child than it is for a typical child. You may find, as we did, that this is an area where your child goes from one extreme to the other. For the longest time, we couldn't seem to get an emotional response out of Grace.

For some parents, the child's inappropriate or absent emotional responses can be a real source of frustration. When Grace started to express her emotions, she *really* started to express her emotions. They would hit her like a tornado, and I was honestly torn between compassion for her upset versus delight that she seemed to have the words and emotions to express herself. I remember chatting with Dr. DeOrnellas about this. She agreed with my gut feeling that Grace was working through these things and that it was not time to sound an alarm. Even though she was, at the time, five years old, this was an area in which her developmental delays were just catching up with her. When a minor disappointment—say, a dropped piece of candy—would cause floods of tears, I would ask myself, "Would I be surprised at this if she were half her age?" Since the answer was no, I wouldn't be surprised to see a two-year-old freak out at losing part of a snack, then my solution, at least initially, is to respond as I would to a two-year-old. Since my child isn't the manipulative type—one of the lovely things about our kids is that they're constitutionally incapable of lying and manipulation—I don't worry about her playing me the way I would with my other kids. As time goes on, I have been proud of how she learns, one step at a time, to manage her emotions. She never gives up! As with so many other tasks, this is harder for her than it is for the average bear, and she shows a lot of character in her persistent progress.

Let me give an example of how my daughter is learning to manage her emotions, and how a parent can help. When Grace was four, I brought her to a birthday party that we thought would be okay; it involved a manageable number of children and no bouncy houses. My husband and I did our best tag-team with the kids, and we left promptly when I started to see the Early Warning Signs—in this case, when our daughter started whining and beginning to withdraw from the group. We got tripped up—literally, as it turned out—by the length of time it took to say our collective goodbyes and get out the door. Even with this frustration, we were able to recover with the help of some downtime together and her favorite snack.

The last thing to be addressed in this chapter is self-injurious behavior (SIB). Although the public is quite aware of these behaviors through television and movies, they are actually fairly rare. However, when they occur, they can be very frightening to parents. SIBs include such things as head-banging, rocking, and biting one's own hands. Siegel (2000) attributes SIBs to an inability to communicate and the accompanying frustration. As children get older and gain some type of language, these behaviors decrease and may disappear altogether. Because higher functioning individuals with ASDs have better language skills, we see few, if any, SIBs.

The light-bulb-crunching incident, as Bobbi so calmly describes it (not always the case), is not what I would consider a true self-injurious behavior. It is more similar to the sensory-seeking behaviors discussed in the previous chapter.

What Exactly Is Going On Inside My Kid's Head?

For the longest time, I just wished someone, anyone, could explain Grace's behavior to me. I totally failed to appreciate the role that anxiety plays in my daughter's life. Grace seems to me to be the happiest, calmest person—except when she is provoked by something that I (mostly) don't understand. What the books of Temple Grandin and many conversations with Dr. DeOrnellas taught me was that much of Grace's behavior is motivated by anxiety. I started to write "inexplicable behavior," but it's quite explicable; I just need to apply myself to learning my child's language. She speaks more with actions than in words, and she doesn't do things just to frustrate or confuse me. She does things for a reason, and if I am respectful of the fact that the reasons are perfectly reasonable to her, I just might learn what that reason is. Speaking of respect, one of the biggest things that I learned from Dr. Grandin's books is the importance of a parent (in her case, her mother) who is willing to be an advocate and never give up.

This chapter is inspired by the following exchange with my daughter just after we started treatment with Dr. DeOrnellas:

Me: Grace, what makes you happy?

G: Someone to play with.

Me: What makes you sad?

G: Nobody to play with.

Me: Who would you like to play with?

(no answer)

Me: Grace, we are going to teach you how to be a friend. Would you like that?

G: Yes, Mama.

Years later, I am happy to report that Grace *does* have friends. For the longest time, this was a great worry of mine. She just didn't seem to connect with other children. What I failed to see is that this wasn't really a worry to Grace. She was, and is, a happy kid. Over time, she has forged her own relationships with siblings and with other children.

Her sixth birthday party was such a happy occasion for me, not only because of the hilarious theme (Raggedy Ann *and* dinosaurs— hey, on your birthday, you get what you want), but because our living room was full of children hand-picked by Grace because they were her friends. Grace has her own timetable and her own ways, and yes, there is a place in the world for her. It's a happy, funny, quirky place. That was a good day. A really, really, good day.

A really, really bad day happened less than a week later. You already know that for every two steps forward, we take at least a step back. We'll call this lesson "Social progress, age six." It's not bad enough that other kids may find your kid to be quirky, nerdy, and withdrawn; after all, that has a certain charm for some. Now add bossy to the mix. Grace has begun to reach out more and more, but has, at the same time, become very, very rigid about her interactions with people. Take a recent hour at the park (was it only an hour?). She wanted to swing only on *that* swing—never mind that someone else was on it, or that it wasn't adjacent to the baby swings where her brother was located. And she wanted *only* Mom to push her, and *only* in a certain way.

Once we navigated that minefield and waited out that sulk, we got to play the bonus round. When three families worth of kids were happily seated around picnic tables eating a snack, she ran off to get a book and then demanded that everyone move to a location of her choosing so that she could read to them. Next thing I knew, I had more than one child in tears.

LUCY ASKS

WHY DID WE HAVE TO LEAVE THE PARK
BECAUSE GRACE THREW A FIT?

Well, Lucy, we had to leave the park because she doesn't understand that:

a. most kids don't come to the park to sit still for story-time; and

b. the ones who are willing to sit still for story-time aren't willing to abandon their snacks to move to a location of her choosing.

There are no simple ways to explain things like "empathy failure" or "communication difficulties" to a small kid. Still, we try.

Parenting Is Like Blow-Drying (Huh?)

Parenting involves the oddest epiphanies. I was chasing Grace around the bathroom recently, trying to blow-dry her hair. She was having the time of her life, because she knew that I was tethered to the dryer cord. I was torn between aggravation at my inability to reach her, worry that she would slip on the bathroom floor and conk her head (again), amusement at her happy giggle, and frustrated amazement that such a simple task could take so long and be so complicated. Finally, I got her to agree to stand still if I would brush her nose instead of her hair, at which point it dawned on me that this was a microcosm of parenting her. Everything that we do with our children is complicated by the labyrinth that we must navigate simply to reach them. Some days, they are just gonna have wet hair. Other days, they'll conk their heads on the floor and we are powerless to stop them. Sometimes, we just have to laugh with them as we brush their noses instead of their hair. It doesn't have to make sense to us.

The Wisdom of the Grace

In fact, I'm learning to look at life a whole 'nother way, as they say, through my kid's eyes. Everybody has their pacifier, the thing that calms them and puts life and its problems at a distance. Some people do yoga. Others drink or take drugs. Still others zone out with the TV, the computer, or food. What if we're all doing these things—some of which can kill you—in pursuit of a peace, a centeredness, a way of *being* that comes naturally to our children? When I observe how *happy* Grace is most of the time, I have to ask myself: Who's the one with the problem here? It's okay to have a pacifier; just make sure it's not poisonous. Allow me to give some examples. A long walk, a hot bath, more hugs, or an extra hour's sleep won't hurt you. On the other hand, excessive use of alcohol, drugs, or food would fall into the "poisonous" category. It's good to get a reality check—and healthy to ask for one—about things

WHAT DR. DeORNELLAS
AND GRACE HAVE TAUGHT ME

IF IT DOESN'T LEND TO THE PEACE OF MY HOME,
THEN IT'S NOT GOOD FOR ANY OF US.

When our kids sometimes do things that are exhausting and upsetting, there is an expert named Dr. Karyn Purvis who may be a great help to you. If you get the chance to read her book, *The Connected Child* (written with Dr. David Cross and Wendy Lyons Sunshine), or to attend any seminar at which she speaks, it's a privilege. While her emphasis is on bonding issues related to adoption, I have found her words and her approach to be very applicable to autism. Part of what I've learned from Dr. Purvis is the importance of looking in the mirror and owning our own stuff. When we are worn out or upset by the behavior of our kids, sometimes the best thing that we can do is stop and ask ourselves, "What do I need here?" I have learned at least as much from my kids as I've taught them. I am not, as the parent, The Finished Product who is here just to teach my kids. I am also a Work in Progress, and the things that push my buttons are often a clue to the areas in which we need to grow right along with our kids.

As I write this paragraph, I have the great privilege of being on an island, far from the stresses of my real life. I'm watching the waves roll in and out, in and out, in anddddd ouuuutttt.... I came here alone, in part in a quest to find out what it feels like to be totally self-contained. On prior trips, I've seen sights, watched whales, hiked, and socialized. But to *just sit* and take in the waves is something else. To see them, hear them, feel them until their rhythm becomes one with the beating of my heart, now that's something I'd never done until now. After a time, my only instinct is to touch the water, to roll in the sand, to be even more alone with the color of the water and the feel of the sand than I already am. This is the gift that my daughter has given to me. Imagine if you experienced everything this way. I can't. And yet, my daughter can't turn it off.

Backwards and in High Heels

Sometimes, when I'm really tempted to lose my cool with my child and scream, *"Why does everything with you have to be so HARD?"* I try to remember how hard it is for HER. She is expected to live and function in a world where *everything* is harder for her than it is for me.

She is expected to mediate with her senses, even though they are calibrated totally differently than mine. She is expected to respond to verbal communication, even though at times she experiences conversations as though they're taking place through an interpreter. She wants friends, but doesn't understand why other kids find some of her behavior off-putting. She has feelings—intense ones—but she frequently encounters people who treat her as if she has none.

Don't get the wrong idea; interacting with these kiddos is no picnic. It can be tough, what with the bossiness, the aggression, the aloofness, the odd behavior. Sometimes, I just have to remind myself that she experiences *everything* differently and she can't explain it to me. When you look at your child's behavior, you may want to remind yourself: this is his normal. Why does your child spin? Maybe it's because she can feel the Earth moving beneath her feet.

Why does he flap? Maybe he can hear the wind singing and he's trying to catch it. Why does he rock? Maybe it reminds him of rocking to sleep inside your womb.

REFERENCES:

American Psychiatric Association. (2000). *Diagnostic and Statistical Manual of Mental Disorders (4th ed., text rev.)*. Washington, DC: Author.

Attwood, T. (2003). Understanding and managing circumscribed interests. In M. Prior (Ed.). *Learning and behavior problems in Asperger's syndrome* (pp. 126-147). New York, NY: Guilford Press.

Chen, Y-H., Rodgers, J., & McConachie, H. (2009). Restricted and repetitive behaviours, sensory processing and cognitive style in children with autism spectrum disorders. *Journal of Autism and Developmental Disorders, 39*, 365-342.

Myles, B. S., & Southwick, J. (1999). Asperger's *syndrome and difficult moments. Practical solutions for tantrums, rage, and meltdowns*. Shawnee Mission, KS: Autism Asperger's Publishing Co.

Siegel, B. (1996). *The world of the autistic child: Understanding and treating autistic spectrum disorders*. New York, NY: Oxford Press.

CHAPTER NINE

Reading, Writing, and Lining Up Her Toys

Different Materials, Different Methods, a Different Pace

As a general statement, kids learn in fits and starts, and their progress is not linear. This is another example of our kids being just like other kids, only more so. When Grace was learning to read, she would do it in enormous surges. I initially used the same methods that I had used with her older sister. Not surprisingly, we didn't exactly proceed along the same path. We used a combination of different resources with Grace, but mostly what she wanted was Real Books, not the phonics method that had worked so well for another child. Being pretty attached to phonics, I had to be creative about working phonics back in, but I couldn't lead with them.

I also want to talk about Grace's progress. For starters, Grace would sometimes go for a month or more in which she seemed to make no progress at all. She would then—usually in conjunction with appalling regressions in seemingly unrelated areas—make enormous surges. She went from zero-to-single-syllable-words-with-short-vowels in just a week or so, while giving us challenges in other areas (remember Chapter Five?) that would make your hair stand on end. A few months later, she did the same thing with the leap to compound words and chapter books.

I Can't Read Your Writing

My research led me to believe that Grace's handwriting was going to lag far, far behind her other skills. It has progressed differently than her other skills, but is going much better than expected. After making it to almost age six as a consistent non-writer, not even forming pre-letter shapes or showing the ability to trace shapes and draw straight or curved lines, she wrote a legible birthday card for Daddy. Was she just keeping her fine penmanship to herself to be coy, or does this skill just pop up from time to time and then go back into hiding? I honestly don't know. I also tried her at occupational therapy for her handwriting and fine motor coordination, but we abandoned that experiment—at least for now—because she is insisting upon doing these things at her own pace. She is now making good progress with her handwriting and steadfastly refusing the ways that I try to help her. As a general rule, her ability to use tools such as pencils and scissors lags far behind her intelligence—not that this has stopped her from playing barber to herself, a sister or two, and a dolly or two.

Working around this challenge is not as hard as it may appear at first. I have begun teach her to type and use the computer much earlier than I otherwise would have. Dry-erase markers, paint, tiny pieces of chalk, little sponges, and manipulatives (blocks, counting bears, and stacking cups) are our current faves.

DR. DEORNELLAS OBSERVES

HEY, GRACE JUST SAVES WRITING FOR SPECIAL OCCASIONS.

Where Do You Go to School?

We have found that a classroom full of other people is not, at this time, the best setting for Grace. In addition to her challenges with completing written work, there are, of course, the social aspects. For now, home schooling works best for us. Simply entering and exiting the building and going through a day's worth of transitions would be an ordeal for her. Plus, where else could she do math in the tub, sometimes for an hour or more? Where else could she sing her reading lessons instead of saying them, or hide between couch cushions while learning? We have tried some classes, co-ops, and activities, but these things are more appropriate for her siblings than they are for Grace. She just finds them too overwhelming, too over-stimulating, too over-everything, even if the groups are small and familiar. In our most recent attempt to ease her into a co-op, we didn't make it half an hour, even with her babysitter and me both by her side. She's made progress, and it wasn't a complete disaster; she just didn't really participate. After her initial elation about being with a group of kids (there are about 100 kids in the co-op and there were maybe a dozen in her class at the time), she didn't participate in any of the activities of the group, and she went from spinning, screeching, and head-butting to "sulking and roaming the perimeter mode."

I freely acknowledge that home schooling isn't going to work for everybody, but it's been terrific for us. We are able to work at Grace's own pace, in every aspect of the day. Sometimes this means spending hours on end reading to her. On the day that this paragraph was written, she trounced me and Mary at a board game until we begged for mercy. Other times, she might do a week's worth of lessons in a day. Or focus on just one subject for several days. Or make no discernable progress for weeks. If she is over stimulated because she was around a lot of people the previous day, it is no big deal for me to hold her and read to her or let her hang out in one of the many small, cozy spaces in our house instead of getting "more useful things" done; that's what I'm there for. We work puzzles and do verbal quizzes and play lots of games involving taking turns—neither of us is very good at taking turns, but we persist. She can also take lots of breaks to swing in the backyard, which helps a lot. I recently asked her if she thought she might like school, and she nonchalantly replied, "No; too much noise, too many people."

I should caution anyone who is considering home schooling a child with special needs to seriously assess the child's needs for stimulation, love, attention, and yes, an education. A great deal of support, as well as curricular and social opportunities, are available, and you shouldn't imagine that you must home school in isolation, or that you would want to.

Changing Subjects

Grace doesn't do transitions well. I don't know that anybody really does, but kids on the autism spectrum have a big challenge with stopping one activity and starting another. I might think that she has worked on a puzzle or read *The Wizard of Oz* for long enough, but—trust me—she doesn't think so. The videos that I mentioned earlier have been a great help, and we do countdowns to transitions as often as we can. Five minute warning to leaving the store! Ten minutes until it's time to brush your teeth! We make these announcements all day long.

CHAPTER TEN

If I've Told You Once, I've Told You a Million Times!

Let Me Entertain You, Let Me Make You Cringe

When we talk about "discipline," we are bound to step on toes. (Didn't I sound just like a social worker in my use of "we" there when I referred to myself?) Let me just apologize to your toes right now and give you my working definition of discipline: for me, it really covers all the different ways that we try to train our kids' minds and hearts and teach them appropriate behavior. In our experience, many of the strategies that work with a NT child are worse than useless in dealing with our kids. You may have a kid who is very rigid or you may have a feral child who doesn't seem to have any self-control or—more typical than you may think—you may have a frustrating combination of both. My purpose in this chapter is to help you to live your life without letting autism be the tyrant that makes both you and your child miserable. Easier said than done, but let's just start where most of our kids start: tantrums.

Meltdowns in Public: Get Used to Humiliation or Stop Leaving Your House

Some days just aren't going to go well. While that's true with any child, I find that I have to remind myself of this often. How do we know if something is an autism thing or a discipline issue?

AS MY HUSBAND (REASONABLY) ASKS

WHO CARES WHICH ONE IT IS?

And how do we manage the response of a sibling who resents what seems to her to be grossly unequal treatment?

LUCY ASKS

DOES GRACE NOT HAVE TO DO THIS CHORE BECAUSE OF AUTISM?

As S. in Oklahoma lamented:

> *What is sensory, what is disobedience? Tolerating possibly too much to avoid a meltdown and the other sibling noticing and wondering why you let them act that way.*

We can have a terrific day that's capped off by my child taking a blunt object to a playmate—or to the bumper of my husband's parked car. For several months, "I wanted to get your attention" was her favorite explanation, as if she hadn't had most of my attention for most of the day. She'll hear a phrase like that, and I'll hear it for months. The next phrase I got, for months on end was, "It was my intent." Huh? Discouraging. Definitely discouraging.

We do our best to try to avoid meltdowns. Sometimes, however, our best efforts do no good. I still cringe when I think of the time that I took four-year-old Grace to a store because I foolishly thought that she needed some one-on-one time after an afternoon at the zoo with her sisters. Yes, she did enjoy the one-on-one time, but the store was overwhelming and violated our One Thing Per Day Rule. This is the perfect example of how something can be both a neurological issue *and* a misbehavior issue at the same time: her behavior was unacceptable (and horrifying), *and* I should have been slapped for trying to have her there at all. A kindly store manager carried out my purchases as I carried out Miss CrabbyPants. That was *after* she had wigged out and thrown things. Not only had I violated our One Thing Per Day Rule, but I also needed a reminder that days do not happen in isolation with us. Each day is influenced by the days that precede and follow. For example, we hunkered down quietly at home for a couple of days before Grace's sister's birthday party, *and* Daddy brought her to the second half of the party in a separate car. The party went very, very well. Lest we pat ourselves on the back, Grace did give us a run for our money the following day when we tried to take her to another function, and we saw to it that the subsequent two or three days were very, very uneventful and included a lot of running around in our backyard to work out the kinks. I am someone who likes nice, clear lines and relationships. I have had to learn to live with the wobbliness of the line between a "discipline issue" and an "autism issue."

As you might imagine, this impacts my relationships with other people as well. I do not hesitate to cancel things at the last minute because Grace just isn't up to going. I have learned the hard way that this is the lesser of the two evils—by a lot. Even if I'm looking forward to it and the tickets are paid for, it's not worth the aggravation to Grace—which she will be sure to share with us, nor is it worth paying the piper for days afterward. This is one of the reasons that it is so important to have a supportive network. By "supportive," I mean a network of people who don't want to kill you when you cancel stuff at the last minute; people who'll forgive you because you'll give them your tickets in exchange for them taking your other kids.

Grace Says "Relax!"

You know those days when you think you're losing your mind—when

You!
Are!
At!
The!
End!
Of!
Your!
Rope!

The next time this happens, just stop everything you're doing. Stop and count to ten, just like Grandma said. Whatever you're doing, it can wait. I promise. (Unless you're driving. Then you need to pull over first.) I'm not going to make you feel worse, honest. Just let me ask you a couple of questions that are designed to help you give your child—and yourself—a break:

- Is your child just overwhelmed? Whatever activity you're doing may just be too much for him. Perhaps he can't do "people stuff" two days in a row. Or for more than an hour at a time.

- Does he really just need to run and climb something? Or bounce? Or be in a corner by himself?

- Are you laughing together enough? (Unless your child is afraid of laughter, and yes, I've heard of that too.)

- Are you expecting too much of him? Yes, I know he's six (or ten, or whatever), but maybe developmentally, he's really half that age.

- Are you seething with anger when what you really need to do is cry? I hereby give you permission. Yes, cry. In privacy if you must. In front of your kid if you need to. For that matter, I don't care who it's in front of. I'm not saying that you need to make this a daily habit, but I'm all for keeping it real.

• Is it time to drop everything and cuddle? Of course, if you have Little Miss Touch-Me-Not, you may have to modify (my kid prefers to be smooshed, except for those times when she doesn't want to be touched at all).

Long story short (as if I ever do that): our kids are a master's-level class in parenting, and the tests always come before the lessons. Get off your own back and hug your kid. If your kid isn't a hugger, hug yourself.

Before we move on, I'd like to say a little about the behaviors Bobbi is describing. Parents typically refer to them as meltdowns or tantrums. To neuropsychologists, they are "catastrophic reactions" (Tantam, 2003, p. 151). I don't hear this term used very often but I think it sums up the situation beautifully. Your child is reacting to something—we often do not know what—in catastrophic proportions (think sinking of the Titanic without the music playing in the background). With older children, we see catastrophic reactions when the child fails at a task or in response to bullying. In younger children, they come most frequently in situations that involve social interaction, such as getting up in the morning, getting into the car to leave the house, being at school (especially during unstructured times like lunch or passing in the halls), and coming home in the evening. They also occur at times when your child's senses are already aroused by being placed in an unfamiliar or unexpected situation. Prevailing wisdom suggests these events are the result of sensory overload—too much light, too much sound, too many people, etc. Being hungry, tired, constipated, retaining urine, or having too much sugar can also spark a catastrophic reaction (Tantam).

When your child is in the midst of a catastrophic reaction, you will typically hear screaming and/or cursing; things will get broken; your child will scratch, hit, or bite himself, or, if you try to restrain him, you are likely to be scratched, hit, or bitten (Tantam, 2003). What can you do? First, and foremost, you must ensure the safety of your child and of anyone else who happens to be close. Then, if your child is safely melting down, reduce stimulation as much as possible. In many cases, this means you must step back and let it happen. It may mean leading a screaming child from a store or a birthday party. This is not the time to talk to him about his behavior. When you do so, he is not hearing you and you are adding to the stimulation. The purpose of his behavior is to escape the cognitive overload he is experiencing. You should only try to contain or confront your child if safety becomes an issue (Tantam).

How Autism Has Turned Us into the Von Trapp Family

As time goes on, we (hopefully) get better at figuring out when Grace is having a teachable moment. I find that I teach my child by repeating myself a lot. A lot. A lot. A lot, lot, lot. You may have already heard the term "social scripts." Dr. DeOrnellas can give you a more comprehensive explanation, but, for me, this means that, every time we are headed to the park, we go over a few key items and rehearse just like a director. Ask lots of leading questions, and be specific. I have also found that the carrot of an incentive generally works better than a threat.

Our social scripts are sung as often as spoken. For whatever reason, singing works better than speaking most of the time. You'd be surprised how many lessons you can set to the tune of "Twinkle, Twinkle, Little Star" when the pressure is on. I've been known to burst into song about the need to hold my hand in a store or to reiterate what is edible and what is not. I am mostly pleased to report that Grace is now doing her own songs from time to time. This is delightful and encouraging—and often funny. We were recently in a restaurant, when Grace announced that she had a song for us, and she began singing "Only eat your food," and inserting the names of the foods that we were eating.

The "social scripts" Bobbi is referring to are similar to Carol Gray's Social Stories™. Ms. Gray, a special education teacher and autism consultant, has written several books describing the Social Story and giving examples. I highly recommend them. When I worked in the schools, we frequently created Social Stories for children who had trouble standing in line, keeping their hands to themselves, washing their hands, using the toilet, managing the lunchroom, etc. I remember creating one with an adolescent that outlined the steps in shaving.

Social Stories work very well with children on the autism spectrum because they help the child establish a routine way of doing something. As we've said, routines are very important. For example, if you are having problems taking your child into a store, one line of the Social Story might be "In the store it's a good idea to keep my hands in my pockets" or "In the store, it is smart to keep one hand on the buggy all the time." Another line might be "In the store, it is not a good idea to ask for things that aren't on the list." Do you see how each line starts with "In the store..."? That repetition is important as a reminder that the behaviors you are asking for are specific to the situation. Read the story to your child (or all your children) prior to each visit to the store or make it into a song and sing it on the way. Soon he will be repeating the words as he goes through the store. This will take a lot of nagging out of your visits and make the experience more pleasant for everyone—including your fellow shoppers.

Social Stories work best when treated as a group activity. Let your child(ren) come up with ideas for lines of the stories. By the time you have taken your child to a store a few thousand times, they know what behavior is expected of them. They just don't always do it. So ask, "What do we do when we go to the store?" "Where do our hands go?" "Do we ask for stuff?" Feed your child the right answers and let him help with making up the story. "Buy-in" is very important. All children are more likely to participate if they feel they had a part in making the rules. It's kind of like democracy but you're really in charge.

By the way, I know from personal experience that Social Stories can be used successfully with many different problem situations. Only recently, however, has there been research to support the use of Social Stories (Ozdemir, 2008; Scattone, Wilczynski, & Edward, 2002.) Scattone et al. found that "when compared to alternate forms of treatment designed to improve social behavior (e.g., discrete trial instruction, pivotal response training, functional equivalence training, etc.), social stories clearly are less time and labor intensive ...." (p. 540). They can also be a lot more fun!

Occasional Success in a Long String of Failures

If I take Grace to a class or other function where she is expected to participate, she may have a tough time for the next couple of days. We see her best behavior when we do the following: let her have at least two hours per day of intense physical activity; minimize screen time; don't worry if she wants to play by herself for what I consider to be long periods of time; have at least an hour of one-on-one continuous interaction with at least one parent each day (and much more when possible) really engaging her—talking with her, walking together, reading, discussing the facial expressions in pictures, etc.; have an early bedtime. She sleeps through the night soundly. We also try to discuss desired behaviors throughout the day, tell her we are proud of her (she requests that we do this and is delighted when we do), and encourage lots of interaction with sisters and friends. We also try to be consistent with rewards and consequences. What constitutes a reward—or a consequence—for our kids may not make any sense at all to other people.

As you've probably already gathered, having one of our kids helps you to get over what other people think. In a hurry. People seem to go to one extreme or the other. Those who wonder why we don't take her out much are just as aggravating as those who can't understand why we ever leave the house with her at all. The truth is that, on any given day, she may or may not be fit for society. And yes, we all have bad days, but how many of your friends have had their four-year-old spin on the floor and foam at the mouth because she finds the lobby of the children's theater overwhelming? (The play was mesmerizing; the problem occurred when she broke concentration and had to be around people who were moving and talking.)

Yes, some days go smoothly, but often I am in the position of trying to control my fear and/or my temper while trying to direct my child, who is mostly oblivious to my efforts. More and more, I am convinced that we have children so that we can grow up. Before children, I can't remember ever even being close to the end of my patience. Seriously. I have many, many weaknesses (most of which you've no doubt already figured out), but I have always been a patient person who could control my emotions. But I am here to tell you, parent to parent, that there is no magical cure that will stop your child from turning into an octopus when you are leaping from one broken heirloom to another at Aunt Sally's. All that you can do in those moments is take a deep breath and concentrate on the safety issues.

It's easy, at the most trying moments, to feel as though you are nose-to-nose with an Impressionist painting. You can't see any beauty when you're that close. It's impossible to even see what you're looking at when you're in the heat of the moment. That's the time—when it's the hardest to do it—that we must, must, must be emotionally smart for two people at the same time. Easier said than done. It's time to step back, count to ten—okay, to a hundred—and make sure that everyone is physically safe from broken pottery or whatever before you try to figure out how to modify your child's behavior. I remember being told that, when you're dealing with a toddler, you have to settle for containment first and then move up the ladder to getting your kid's attention and eventually working with him to change his behavior. When I begin to wonder if I'm ever going to get this parenting thing right, I have to remember that sequence: first, containment, then move up the ladder. Remember the mom earlier in the book who told us that things got easier once we stopped expecting our kids to be normal? It's very applicable when it comes to behavior. You may have a kid who looks like a nine-year-old, but acts like a two-year-old. You have to deal with the two-year-old in front of you, even if he is taller than you are.

Also, quit blaming yourself. I know, gentle reader, that you do. If there is one thing that Grace and Dr. DeOrnellas have conspired to teach me, it is that no effort of mine, however marvelous, is going to change the fact that my child deals with special challenges that put a lot of wear and tear on me. Accepting this is a great gift that you can give to yourself. Having said that, yes, we do need to guide our children or at least get their attention. I call this "finding their price."

Finding Grace's price—both positively and negatively—is a merry chase that never ends. Just for grins, I'll give you some examples. These examples may well be worthless to you, because they certainly are no longer of any use to us. For a period of time, the only thing that would motivate Grace was for Daddy to threaten that he wouldn't let her look out the window and wish on a star at bedtime. Unfortunately for me, this only worked when coming from him. For a period of time, the key to stopping Grace's misbehavior was to hold her firmly in our arms with her arms at her sides; since then, she's decided that being held like that is the niftiest thing in the world; she'll actually ask for it. She likes to keep us on our toes. In her books, Dr. Temple Grandin gives the example of the babysitter who would pop a paper bag in her face if she didn't focus on her dinner.

I'm getting better at spotting teachable moments. Grace once came howling down the stairs near bedtime, lamenting the fact that she had trashed all of her wooden nutcrackers. Call it a sensory thing, but the child loved to sleep with hard, wooden, 24-inch nutcracker figurines. She also liked to play with them in ways that cost them limbs, noses, and even square, wooden bases. It had suddenly occurred to her that she had none of them left. Nor did she have a single piece of the nesting nutcrackers that I had given to her just a couple of weeks before. I held her in my lap like a baby and encouraged her to cry. I also took an opportunity to teach a little empathy. I said something like, "Honey, it's good that you are feeling sad because you loved your nutcrackers and the sadness will help you remember to be more gentle to your nutcrackers if you get any more of them. The way you feel right now—that's how Mommy feels when you cut up the sheets." The look on her face went from grief to pure astonishment. If there was a "eureka!" bubble above my head, there was an even bigger one over her head that said, "REALLY?" I have also used similar strategies to help her understand that other people feel pain. My daughter, who was once oblivious to the most awful physical insults, experiences a shower (of any temperature) like a torrent of icy knives. This was also a good lesson in not getting insulted by the fact that things are often more important to her than people.

MY DUH! MOMENT

I HAVE PURCHASED A STUFFED, SOFT NUTCRACKER
FOR GRACE TO SLEEP WITH. SHE NAMED HIM DAVID.
AS OF THIS WRITING, DAVID HAS SURVIVED
FOR MORE THAN A YEAR.

These learning opportunities also present themselves in other areas; I have leveraged this knowledge to teach her that other people feel pain too. "Honey, you know the way that feels to you? That's the way it feels to little Dottie Waxbean when you body-slam her/pull out handfuls of her hair/whatever."

Idiot-Proofing

Legend has it that prior generations of moms fanned out the magazines and knick-knacks on the glass-top table and Junior never touched them, but let's face it: it's really easier to tailor the environment. Plus, our generation of parents is notably less willing to beat our children than generations past, so it really is easier to just eliminate temptation. This goes double for a child who seems to be training for a future in the circus.

Even though baby gates barely slowed my children down, there are still a lot of things that we can do. We have an alarm system, if for no other reason than it chirps when an exterior door or window is opened. All of our exterior doors (and some of our interior ones) feature super-duper childproof locks that our kids can't reach (at least not yet). Low cabinets can be stocked with plastics, pans, and other unbreakables.

I recently came across a "to-do" list that I wrote for my handyman in early 2008. No joke. Every single item relates to one child. Here is what I wrote:

Could you please:
- Re-attach mesh on upstairs banisters and railings
- Figure out which sprinkler heads are smashed and replace them
- Put knobs back on dresser and fix broken drawers
- Fix holes in sheetrock and put hooks back up in downstairs bathroom
- Fix broken baby gate
- Re-bolt bookshelf to wall
- Fix Ben's sit-up machine
- Reassemble shoe-keeper (it has been climbed on)

Breaking It Down

There are lots of things that come intuitively to you that are a complete mystery to your child. Logically, this is going to cause your child a lot of frustration. Understanding this will help you to teach her. If your child seems to be blowing you off, it may just mean that you aren't speaking her language and you need to break things down into bite-sized pieces so that she can digest them.

For example, Temple Grandin has written an amazing book called *Unwritten Rules of Social Relationships* that includes important information that might be intuitive to you or me, but which needs to be explained to our kids. For example, she explains their difficulty in reading faces and she goes into a lot of detail about how this can create awkward, job-threatening or even dangerous situations for an autistic person. She also explains how literal and trusting that autistic folks can be, and she tells them things like: Not everyone who is nice to you is your friend. I don't know about you, but that's a lesson we all could use. Please don't take my word for it; *Unwritten Rules of Social Relationships* is an important book that you should read for yourself.

WHAT I WISH I'D KNOWN

WE DO THIS FOR OURSELVES, AND OUR TYPICAL KIDS, ANYWAY;
IT'S JUST A DIFFERENT WAY WITH THESE KIDS.
THINK OF IT AS CUTTING A SANDWICH WITH A COOKIE CUTTER
INSTEAD OF A BUTTER KNIFE. IT'S STILL THE SAME SANDWICH.

Now You See Her, Now You Don't

I have a child who is fond of climbing and disappearing. It's a paradox: the child who *seems* to want the least attention actually needs my attention the most. It only takes a moment's inattention in a place like a mall to totally lose sight of our kids. Now, I know that some of you are saying, "Yeah, but that's true of every child, isn't it?" Yeah, when they're two. You don't expect it from kids who are six and older, but many of our children are experts at making themselves invisible, and let's just say that the two-year-old phase of running away in the parking lot is lasting a LOT longer with one of my children than it did with the others.

In *A Slant of Sun,* the author tells the story of her little boy disappearing. I have to tell you, this story was so close to the bone with me—and so sensitively told—that it made me cry. Keeping our kids safe can be a draining ordeal. While Grace isn't a runner (anymore), she went through a two-year period in which she would intermittently decide that her seatbelt really wasn't necessary. I consider this to be a Very Awful Problem. I think that the interior of the minivan is just too cavernous for her sometimes because she never does it in our sedan. My kids stayed in the biggest, sturdiest car-seats, complete with five-point harnesses, that I could find, until they really, really outgrew them. I initially purchased these because I was a Nervous Nellie about safety (I say *was* because my fears turned out to be reasonable), but we keep them now because our child doesn't need to be in a car seat or seatbelt from which she can remove herself (her fine motor coordination has not kept pace with her climbing ability or her fearlessness). Think of it as idiot-proofing. (Please don't think that I'm calling your child an idiot; I'm referring to *parents* here.) My patience does not extend to risking death on the highway. I have to pull over, get out of the car, count to ten, and get her safe. If it's any consolation, I have heard similar stories from parents of neurologically typical children from time to time.

Many of her dangerous behaviors made no sense to me because I couldn't see the appeal. For example, when she was almost five, Grace had a brief romance with the control button for our overhead garage door opener. While her siblings were very willing to heed my (emphatic) insistence that they a) NEVER touch it, and b) run away from the garage door itself any time that it is moving,

Grace wasn't tuned in to those admonitions; she and that garage door opener took years off the end of my life.

I've heard of parents who have smashed a tomato with the garage door to make their point, but I feared that this would just excite her more. Grace seemed so delighted and fascinated with making the garage door move that she was utterly oblivious to the danger that this posed to herself and her siblings. When people laugh at the childproof locks on most of the doors in our house, they just aren't aware of challenges like this. As for me, I do what has become routine: repeat myself *ad nauseum,* watch like a hawk, do everything I can to mitigate the danger (including enhancing the childproofing around that area EVEN FURTHER and ratcheting up consequences for Grace if she so much as looks at that control button), and tell myself that these fascinations usually only last a couple of weeks. Or a couple of months. Fortunately, Grace is once again ignoring the garage door opener. Long may it last, I say.

WHAT I WISH I'D KNOWN

I HAD NO IDEA HOW TO MOTIVATE OR DETER
MY CHILD WHEN I DIDN'T KNOW HER SENSITIVITIES.
WE WENT TO DESPAIR AND BACK SO MANY TIMES,
THINKING WE'D NEVER FIND HER PRICE, WHEN WE JUST
HAD TO PUT OURSELVES IN HER SHOES AND THINK LIKE HER.

B obbi touched on the problem of elopement, which is much less romantic that it sounds. Elopement (running away) is a serious problem with some children on the autism spectrum. It is typically seen in preschoolers who lack the verbal skills to say "I gotta get out of here." However, I have seen it in elementary age children and in a sixteen-year-old who jumped out of a moving car on the Pennsylvania Turnpike. With elementary age children, I have seen Special Education teachers appoint an aide to be in charge of guarding the door because a particular child has a penchant for running down the hall to the outside door.

Whatever the age, elopement is very scary to parents and anyone else who happens to witness it. A child may dart into traffic or into the arms of a stranger. The key to solving the problem of elopement lies in figuring out when the child runs. Sometimes it is during less structured times, while in others, it is during times of increased demand, such as during academic instruction (Perrin, Perrin, Hill, & DiNovi, 2008). See below for the ABCs of behavior analysis. Once we know when a child runs, we can start to figure out why. It may be to avoid a task that is unpleasant or to escape a situation that is overwhelming. Unpleasant tasks can be completed by pairing them with pleasurable activities. Ten minutes of picking up means five minutes of computer time (or whatever is reinforcing to your child). Overwhelming situations are best overcome by avoiding them altogether or exposure to them in small increments.

Saying the Un-sayable

There are some things that we'd rather not talk about, namely fear. Remember the story about the boy bashing Mom's head against the faucet in Chapter One? What about being a little bit afraid of your own child? One mom—and she's not the only one—described how she felt "physically threatened" by her eleven-year-old:

There have been a few times I've thought he was going to hit me, and once he threatened to stab me six times in my sleep. Please note that therapist number four told me this was NOR-MAL and that clearly I didn't love him enough.

— J., Massachusetts

I should add that this parent displayed particular insight into her child's condition, stating that he was *"trying to live colorblind or with no depth perception, or in a foreign country where he only understands half the language."* This is a reality to be faced head-on, not a cause for embarrassment or shame. This is where professional help comes in handy (to put it mildly). You may also benefit from keeping track of triggers that may seem insignificant to you, but are anything *but* insignificant to your child. For example, I have observed that there is a certain time of year that we find particularly challenging. I don't really understand *why;* I can just use this insight to be very vigilant, extra attentive and loving, and to cut out any avoidable stressors during that time.

I'll Cry If I Want To

Part of what we need to do is to let go of the fantasy of the perfect child and perfect family. It's painful and embarrassing to realize that I've even harbored such fantasies, much less to let go of them. While this is true to some extent with any child, our children give us extra opportunities. When my husband and I were dating, I remember telling him that I didn't want to take the children to church without him. Turns out that, for me, the Perfect Family Picture included attending church together. Life has a funny way of coming along and saying, Ding! Thank you for playing.

Let me just end this chapter with the picture of a tearful mom on Christmas Eve realizing that she and her husband must, in the future, take turns taking *some* of the children to Mass. (You may also want to picture the other parishioners, who are not tearful, or even reverent, but rather pissed off at a certain family.) We try to think of it as just another opportunity to take care of each other.

155

A lot of children with ASDs have problem behaviors. These are in addition to the catastrophic reactions discussed earlier in this chapter. Anxiety, depression, mood swings, severe irritability, phobic symptoms or social phobia, Attention-Deficit/Hyperactivity Disorder (ADHD), epilepsy, aggression, self-injurious behaviors (from head-banging to jumping out of moving cars to eating light bulbs), and stereotypical behaviors are all more common in this population. As a result, nearly half of all children with ASDs are on psychotropic medications, including atypical antipsychotics (Lecavalier, Gadow, DeVincent, & Edwards, 2009).

Why do they have these behaviors?

Many theories have been offered—genetics, brain chemistry, poor parenting, diet, etc. Love, Carr, and LeBlanc (2009) suggest that "the combination of impaired social and language skills and restricted interests often lead to the development of other problem behaviors" (p. 363). This sounds right to me, especially when we are talking about aggressive behavior. Aggression is one of the greatest concerns that parents bring to me. Aggressive children are poorly tolerated by peers, siblings, teachers, and parents of other children—particularly as the child gets older and larger.

Tantam discussed the displacement of aggression in children with ASDs (2003). When a child has a bad day at school or is bullied on the playground, he lacks the skills to express his anger in words. He holds it in until a safe target (one that will not retaliate) emerges. The target is typically his mother or siblings and they are caught off guard by this aggression since they have not done anything to the child to warrant it.

Before you can figure out how to stop the problem behaviors, it is important to know what is triggering them. A functional behavioral assessment is used to determine what is happening in your child's world (A) that caused him to have a behavior (B) and what the consequences of that behavior were (C). In more technical language, the antecedent (A) is followed by the behavior (B) which is followed by the consequence (C).

For children not on the autism spectrum, the following might occur:

Johnny goes to school. While walking through the hall, Damien pushes Johnny (A), Johnny pushes him back (B), and both boys get detention (C).

The same scenario could have a different ending:

Johnny goes to school, Damien pushes him (A), Johnny tells a teacher (B), and Damien gets detention (C). Johnny is praised by the teacher for doing the right thing (C).

These scenarios are acted out every day at home or school. Most children can see that the second scenario works out better for them and they can be encouraged to tell the teacher or a parent if something happens to them. They learn that aggression, although it may be the first impulse, is wrong and should be avoided.

With children on the autism spectrum, a functional behavioral assessment can be a lot trickier. For example:

Janie goes to school and Tiffany makes fun of her (A), Janie doesn't know what to say to Tiffany but she feels bad. She thinks about it all day long but still doesn't know what to say. By the time she gets home from school, Janie is very angry and hits her mother (B). Janie's mother is taken by surprise, yells at Janie, and sends her to her room (C).

In this case, our antecedent is very clear. If Janie had retaliated with Tiffany by pushing her or saying something equally insulting, we would not condone the behavior but we would understand it. The consequence that resulted would "fit the crime." In this case, however, Janie held on to her anger and thought about it all day. She lacked the language and social skills to tell a teacher or to say something to Tiffany. By the time she got home, she was ready to explode and we have an example of the misplaced and delayed aggression discussed earlier. Mom represents a safe target. Mom also reinforced Janie's behavior in two ways. First, she reinforced it by giving Janie attention—she yelled at her. Secondly, she reinforced Janie by sending her to her room. After a stressful day at school, going to her room was exactly what Janie needed.

Behavior that is reinforced is likely to be repeated. Most behavior (yours, mine, your child's) is maintained by social reinforcement. For children with ASDs, that social reinforcement almost always comes from caregivers because they have not developed the ability to gain access to social reinforcement in an appropriate way from peers (Love et al., 2009).

So, what do we do with the information we have learned in our functional behavioral assessment? As parents, you are the expert on your child. If your child is in a public school—no matter how wonderful it is—your child is going to be stressed when she gets home. Recognize that and plan accordingly. Don't pepper her with questions the minute she gets in the car or walks through the door. Give her alone time in a safe, secure place (i.e., in the closet, listening to music with headphones, swinging, jumping on a trampoline, etc.). Give her a chance to unwind from the sensory overload (this works great for parents, too). Later, you can ask how her day went and use this time for teachable moments. Janie's mother can rehearse with her a suitable comeback or a behavior that will limit the insults. Also, Janie's mother can be vigilant with regard to bullying and report Tiffany's behavior to school officials.

One more thing. As I previously stated, nearly half of children with ASDs are on some type of medication intended to control their mood and/or their behavior. Making that decision is extremely difficult for most parents. On the one hand, there is hope that medication will make their child reachable and teachable; on the other hand, there is fear their child will be forever changed or harmed by the effects of medication we barely understand. We need more research into the appropriate medications for children on the autism spectrum. We also need more time to learn about the long-range effects of these medications.

There has not been a great deal of research into the use of psychotropic (also known as psychoactive) drugs with children, especially with children with ASDs. Psychotropic drugs are those that have an effect on psychological processes like thinking, feeling, and perceiving. Stigler and McDougle (2008) looked into the use of pharmacotherapy (i.e., using drugs as treatment) for severe irritability in children with ASDs. They reported that Risperidone (marketed as Risperdal) is the only atypical antipsychotic approved for use with children with ASDs. Olanzapine (Zyprexa) and Aripiprazole (Abilify) are currently being studied. Guanfacine (Tenex) has been found to be helpful for children with Asperger's disorder. Anticonvulsants and mood stabilizers have not been found to be helpful. For more information, see Leskovec, Rowles, and Findling (2008). They reviewed a number of drug studies using children and adolescents with ASDs.

In conclusion, the decision to use psychotropic medications with your child is a personal decision. This decision should be made with input from a physician you trust (preferably a child psychiatrist who works with children with ASD). Psychotropic medications are powerful agents that should only be used for moderate to severe behavior problems that have not responded well to behavioral treatment alone. Research is currently being conducted into the use of behavioral intervention with Risperidone (Scahill, 2008). I believe the results will indicate that a combination of treatments will be more effective than medication alone.

References:

Lecavalier, L., Gadow, K. D., DeVincent, C. J., & Edwards, M. C. (2009). Validation of DSM-IV model of psychiatric syndromes with autism spectrum disorders. *Journal of Autism and Developmental Disorders, 39,* 278-289.

Lescovec, T. J., Rowles, B. M., & Findling, R. L. (2008). Pharmacological treatment options for autism spectrum disorders in children and adolescents. *Harvard Review of Psychiatry, 16,* 97-112.

Love, J. R., Carr, J. E., & LeBlanc, L. A. (2009). Functional assessment of problem behavior in children with autism spectrum disorders: A summary of 32 outpatient cases. *Journal of Autism and Developmental Disorders, 39,* 363-372.

Ozdemir, S. (2008). The effectiveness of Social Stories on decreasing disruptive behaviors of children with autism: Three case studies. *Journal of Autism and Developmental Disorders, 38,* 1689-1696.

Perrin, C. J., Perrin, S. H., Hill, E. A., & DiNovi, K. (2008). Brief functional analysis and treatment of elopement in preschoolers with autism. *Behavioral Interventions, 23,* 87-95.

Scahill, L. (2008). How do I decide whether or not to use medication for my child with autism? Should I try behavior therapy first? *Journal of Autism and Developmental Disorders, 38,* 1197-1198.

Scattone, D., Wilczynski, S. M., Edwards, R. P. & Rabian, B. (2002). Decreasing disruptive behaviors of children with autism using social stories. *Journal of Autism and Developmental Disorders, 32,* 535-543.

Tantam, D. (2003). Assessment and treatment of comorbid emotional and behavior problems. In M. Prior, (Ed.), *Learning and behavior problems in Asperger's syndrome* (pp. 148-174). New York, NY: Guilford Press.

CHAPTER ELEVEN

My Child and Other People

Ya Gotta Have Friends

Confucius said: "Silence is the true friend that never betrays." Perhaps Confucius had an ASD? He was very intelligent, after all ... but I digress (again). Our children appreciate solitude on a level that most of us never will. Our kids don't socialize the way that typical kids do—when they socialize at all. I don't know about you, but I've wasted a lot of energy worrying about my child's social life, or lack thereof. Really, we shouldn't get ourselves so worked up; we'll have so many other opportunities.

While our kids can get frustrated by realizing that they are different, they don't experience social interactions the way that we do, and I am willing to bet that we worry much more about this than they do. My observations were a lot like this parent's:

He doesn't seem to understand ordinary social interactions. Watching him try to interact with friends is like watching a deaf person try to dance: he knows the moves but doesn't know where they go. He resorts to trying to order people around.

— J., MASSACHUSETTS

Your child's definition of "friend" may not be the same as yours— and it may surprise you. I could totally relate to J., in Ohio, who tells us:

He doesn't really have close friendships and yet he never says one word about needing any. He is okay with kids for the most part as long as they don't over-extend themselves when he's had enough. He usually plays with other kids for only about an hour before he needs a break. He takes one and then comes back and is fine. He has one playmate that he will tell he needs a break, but his friend just doesn't understand so our son ends up having a meltdown. We typically stay very involved with him when he's around others, because a few times, I've caught him getting ready to hit. He seems to do well as long as he's allowed to have his own space when he needs it.

I think this is an area in which we parent-types suffer much more than our kids do. Now would be a good time to let Dr. DeOrnellas tell you about her research in this area.

It's true that children with ASDs do interpret friendship differently. When we asked sixty-seven children and adolescents with high-functioning ASDs about their friends, each one was able to name several friends. When we followed up with their parents, most had never heard of these friends. If they had, it was someone their child sat next to in class or in the lunchroom. We also asked the same children to rate their social skills—all believed they had adequate skills and were doing fine—none reported significant social skills deficits. Their parents, on the other hand, rated their skills as being very low.

This begs the question of whether or not children with ASDs feel lonely. Do they understand friendship as we do? Bauminger and Kasari (2000) explored those questions with a group of twenty-two children with high-functioning ASDs. They found that these children did feel lonely but their understanding of loneliness was not the same as that of other children. There are two aspects to loneliness: an emotional dimension and a social-cognitive dimension. The emotional dimension includes the feelings we experience when we are lonely (i.e., sad, restless, fearful, empty). The social-cognitive dimension requires us to compare our situation to that of others. We notice that other people are in relationships or belong to a group, and we feel excluded. We may also feel bored or that our lives are meaningless. In other words, "loneliness is linked to a basic ability to know about relationships and to feel and experience emotions" (Bauminger & Kasari, p. 447). When asked to define loneliness, the children in their study frequently omitted the emotional aspect of loneliness and were twice as likely to include the social-cognitive dimension. "It may be that children with autism have difficulties relating "feelings" to their "knowledge" of loneliness (Bauminger & Kasari, p. 453).

In the Bauminger and Kasari study, all twenty-two of the children with high-functioning ASDs reported having a best friend, yet less than 10% were able to give a complete definition of friendship (2000). Children with ASDs do not interpret friendship in the same way that other children do. I have had a child tell me their best friend is Jamie—only to learn that Jamie is the one child who doesn't make fun of him. Jamie hasn't made an overture of friendship—he just hasn't been mean. Since the friendships of children with ASDs do not typically include the intimacy, emotion, or companionship that are the hallmarks of friendship, it is possible that their loneliness is due to the poor quality of their friendships rather than to a lack of friendships.

Interestingly, Bauminger and Kasari (2000) found that mothers of the children in their study reported twice as many friends for their children as they reported for themselves. However, they tended to talk about desired rather than actual relationships and the activities their children engaged in with friends required little social interaction. This is similar to the results we found with the parents in our study. The child with ASD reported having a best friend but that friend would probably consider their relationship an acquaintanceship rather than a friendship. In addition, playing video games, which requires few interactions, appears to be the activity of choice for most children with ASDs and their friends.

In a more recent study, Bauminger, Solomon, Aviezer, Heung, Brown, and Rogers (2008) looked more closely at the friendships of children with high functioning ASDs. They looked at "mixed" dyads, which included a child with ASD and a friend with typical development, and "non-mixed" dyads in which both children had an ASD. They found pros and cons to both types of friendships. Mixed friendships more closely resembled friendships between typically developing children. Their play was more coordinated, the children had more fun together, and they appeared to have a closer relationship. The friendship lasted longer and the friends were more responsive to each other. However, there was an imbalance of power as the child with ASD was less likely to take a leadership role. In non-mixed friendships, the children were more likely to take turns being the leader, which was important for promoting self-esteem and learning social skills (Bauminger et al.). These friendships can be easier to orchestrate in that parents may be more likely to make the effort to ensure the children get together regularly.

In my experience, children with ASDs do not experience the sadness we associate with loneliness but they do recognize that they are being left out of things. This is especially true at school where children frequently divide into dyads or small groups on the playground or for group projects. Most children want to be a part of the group and realize when they are missing out on something. I have also found that parents play an important role in helping their children to make friends. Parents who have friends frequently can negotiate play dates with the children of their friends. Because the parents have a relationship, the children are more likely to see each other more than once and a level of comfort can develop. It is also important to encourage your child to have friendships by modeling the behaviors of friendship. Involving them in activities that allow for social interaction such as playing board games, cooking, or crafts will go further in establishing relationships than the parallel play of videogames.

Look on the Bright Side

You may be afraid that some folks will be put off by your child's uniqueness. What you may not yet know is that there will be friends who are friends *because* of your child's uniqueness.

My biggest worry is that he will never understand the rules of society and I don't know if he will ever really experience truly loving someone. I don't know how to teach the feeling of love. All I can do is show him my unconditional love for him and hope in time he will understand.

— L., TEXAS

Grace has, within the past year, formed a lovely friendship with another little girl who is also on the autism spectrum. The two of them found each other in a sporting activity involving several dozen other people. As it happens, the other girl's mother is also a lot of fun, so we are all very pleased. It is a lovely mystery to me how these two kids found each other. Sometimes they happily play for a long period of time without speaking or even looking at each other. Recently, when they encountered each other at a birthday party, Grace showed her joy by hugging her friend and then doing four laps around the room while her friend smiled and watched.

Even when they weren't interacting directly (okay, what I would consider to be direct—I should know better by now), they were each just so happy that the other one was there.

Grace constantly inspires us to see the world in a different way. Often, this is delightful, and there's a lot that we could miss if we were only seeing things our way. Last year, we took Grace to a Brazilian chiarascurria—you know, one of those restaurants where they walk around with meat on a skewer and they cut it off onto your plate with enormous knives?? She basked in the experience of being on a special outing with Mom and Dad, with no siblings in tow, and she showed a surprising willingness to try new foods, within reason (especially if we told her that they had garlic salt on them). She also informed the waiters that they seemed all set to defend the restaurant with their swords and skewers if it were attacked by wolves or bandits.

I'll Be the Princess; You Be the Horse. Again.

I am surprised to have to manage matters large and small. Grace, who is truly a peaceful soul, will suddenly throw her sister from a chair ("She was in my seat") or clothesline her as she passes her in the hallway ("I wanted to be there"). She doesn't instinctually understand that a person in her way is more than an object to be eliminated. She also isn't going to take too kindly to someone sitting in Her Seat, no matter who that someone is or how embarrassed Mom may be at Grace's way of expressing herself.

Any smart parent knows that you can't mediate your children's relationships with each other. Any protective parent knows that you can't sit back and do nothing when one of your children is torturing a sibling. Finding the balance between these two things can feel like nailing Jell-o to a wall. My kids love to dress up and play pretend, and I've had to learn not to intervene when Grace wants to wear her lion costume for days in a row, or when her sister casts herself in the starring role every time. Many's the time I've said something like, "No, you can't make Grace be the tree again," only to realize that Grace is a happy little tree, having a perfectly good time. Parenting gets a lot easier when I remember that my kids have their own tastes and preferences. Grace's older sister has also benefited from reading *Russell is Extra Special: A Book About Autism for Children*, a picture book that Dr. Charles Amenta wrote about his son.

Buh-Bye to the Playgroup

Through painful experience, I have learned that Grace just doesn't do well with more than about an hour with a group of other kids. Sometimes, I just decide it's not worth the stress to even try.

> *Sometimes I just want to sit back and chitchat with other people instead of being on the lookout for the spark that starts the outburst.*
>
> — R., ILLINOIS

Around the time Grace turned four, I got involved in a weekly playgroup with a handful of other families. We would get together for playdates, or one of the moms would read aloud and lead the kids in a simple craft. You know, things involving Popsicle sticks, edible paste, and a total loss of parental dignity. Anyway, my daughter would do great for the story time part, maybe sever one of my fingers with the safety scissors during the craft, but then, as the one-hour-mark approached, she'd turn into a really manic pumpkin. Maybe she'd run headlong into my arms first. Then she'd run that way to one of the other moms. Next, it would be one of the six-year-old boys, who thought that was great fun. The two-year-olds, not so much. I found that, once she got wound up to that degree, it took a day or more to really get her back to her Happy Place. Reluctantly, I started getting a sitter while I took my other kids. I felt tremendous guilt: I was leaving her at home! Was I punishing her for something that wasn't her fault? Dr. DeOrnellas gently suggested that, given what I had observed, maybe continuing to bring her was really the punishment. (Certainly it felt that way to Mom.) The reality was that Grace enjoyed a couple of hours of our sitter's undivided attention and the other kiddos and I got a bit of socializing.

Some kids on the spectrum need a lot of downtime to recover after being in a social situation. Others need a lot of time to "wind down" after a meltdown.

> *He goes volcanic very quickly, and it's hard to diffuse the situation before he gets to that point. It's as if he trips a switch and then has to run the tantrum to the end before he can get his cool back.*
>
> — J., MASSACHUSETTS

We try to prevent meltdowns by limiting the time of social engagements. Sometimes our One-Hour-Pumpkin Rule seems silly to others, but it has served us well. If she's at home, outdoors, or with familiar people, she can handle a longer play-date. If she's tired or the setting is unfamiliar or we're dealing with a cast of thousands, it can be a lot less.

Sometimes, the best-laid plans just don't get you there. Sometimes you and your child can enjoy a party. A small party, not too long, in a familiar setting, without too many sensory triggers, hosted by sensitive and understanding friends. Even with all of those precautions, you may still find yourself leaving early because your child has become overwhelmed and Done What He Does When He Does What He Does—physically attacked someone, spun until something broke or just weirded people out. Learning to take such events in stride and remove oneself and one's child (at least to a bathroom) is just part of the joy of being us. You do all that you can to make things work, and sometimes they do.

I also don't recommend any indoor sports like basketball, where people are expected to collide and the acoustics of the room would be excruciating. As I've learned, what is painful to her is soon going to become painful to the rest of us. Very, very painful. Over time, Grace and I both learned to recognize the early warning signs and get the heck outta Dodge no matter what thrill we might be missing. I am proud of her for beginning to manage this along with me.

Sometimes she will ask for me to squeeze her tightly when we are in an unfamiliar setting. Sometimes she will recognize that she needs to be alone and go to one of her favorite spots—usually the dollhouse inside our playroom. If she shuts the door, the rest of the family knows to respect that and leave her alone. After fifteen minutes or so, I will typically go in and ask her how it's going. Even this conversation tends to be a little scripted.

T. M. I.

The word "information" brings up another question: how much information is Too Much Information? How do we alert others to what they may see from our kids without freaking them out and making them think that we are just crazy helicopter parents, hovering over our apparently "normal" children? On the other hand, how much information does someone have a right to know before dropping off their child at my house? Personally, I resolved this dilemma by writing a book. For the rest of you, I'd recommend a balanced approach. Initially, I'm sure that I erred on the side of over-sharing. Now, I try to calibrate the information I give to the situation. Time also has a way of helping, because most of the people that we encounter on a regular basis are well-acquainted with Grace and her issues. That's okay—I know the weird stuff about their kids too, and I still like 'em. Even so, the most understanding friends really don't want my child throwing their child off the swing set.

For purposes of both disclosure and safety, you may want to think about getting a MedicAlert bracelet for your kid. Our priest recommended this after we explained Grace's situation to him. It is a visible sign that there is a challenge that may not be immediately obvious, and we pray that we never have to "use" it, but it is comforting to know that if Grace were separated from us in a situation where she needed help, emergency personnel would at least be able to understand her communication difficulties and be able to reach us immediately. We let her pick out the design. She calls it her Princess Power bracelet and she tells us that it keeps her safe.

Nobody else in our house has a Princess Power bracelet. Some of us are very, very jealous. Especially Lucy. And me.

Finding Friends Who Aren't Afraid of Your Kids

Remember my lovely moment at the beach a couple of chapters ago? The thing is, I don't live at the beach. Back to the real world. Brushing a child's nose or worrying much more than she does about her social life is one thing; keeping her safe is another. I completely related to L. in California who told me the following about her young child:

> *K was very impulsive. Very object-oriented and not people-oriented. Sometimes living things like animals or people were treated like objects and she'd grab at them in ways that weren't respectful. If I felt the animal or person could be harmed I always had to act quickly to intercept the speed at which she'd grab or do something. It always looked like I had not prepared her for these situations and that I continued to not discipline K for her actions. In truth, repetition and role-playing were constant but the results did not "stick." The lesson or talk would be repeated as if the previous one hadn't happened. [It] embarrassed me to be seen in public with the behavior my child exhibited. I started to doubt my parenting abilities and the bad attention we got in public places made it even worse. Shame, frustration, and embarrassment were daily feelings.*

What got us into treatment was that our child was a danger to herself and others. It was the "others" part that really got our attention. Somehow we felt that, as her parents, we could and should protect her, but she got so *extroverted* with the dangerous stuff. Whether she was yanking off Daddy's glasses without warning or climbing on top of the minivan in a single bound, we often didn't see it coming. Part of the pain of parenting a child with these kinds of differences is the illusion that you can make it all okay.

Another problem is that, to the casual observer—that is, the one whose glasses aren't getting yanked off—your child *looks* just like any other child.

Quality, Not Quantity

Temple Grandin writes, in several of her books, about her choice to remain single and the fact that her satisfying social interactions arise from shared interests in common work. Reading this, along with knowing the results of Dr. DeOrnellas' research, helps me to understand that this is Yet Another Area in which our kids really are just like other kids, but more so.

There are all kinds of play therapies, and some of them just might work. Your child may actually come up with some of them herself. Grace has been known to use inanimate objects as translators, and she has had some conversations with kids who aren't very verbal this way. She'll use a toy—a doll, a pumpkin—as a translator of sorts. "Hey, Pumpkin! Ask Fred if he wants to throw you at me." At Christmastime that year, she carried a three-foot wooden snowman around with her and we used him to have some lovely conversations until she broke him in half. Too bad he didn't make it through Advent. She was much more fluent in conversation with me—especially responding to my questions—with Frosty as a go-between.

There is a lovely quote attributed to C. S. Lewis that applies to our kids just as much as any others: "Friendship is born at that moment when one person says to another: 'What! You, too? Thought I was the only one.'"

Grace's relationship with her infant brother has been a wonder to behold. They communicate just fine. He thinks that she is the funniest person in the house and she never, ever gets tired of playing Peekaboo. One of his first words was her name.

I recently witnessed a tender scene in which my Grace and a five-year-old boy played together by throwing toy cars and puzzle pieces at one another. Grace actually made conversation, sort of. It went sort of like this:

Throw, throw, throw

She: "That's my mom over there. Her name is Bobbi."

Throw, throw, throw.

She: "My dad's name is Ben."

(Ten minutes of uninterrupted throwing, followed by a pause while Grace reacts to car hitting face.)

Throw, throw, throw

She thought that was the best time *ever*. When I asked her later if she had enjoyed playing with him, she said, with a big smile, "Oh, yes, the puzzle pieces didn't go in a straight line!"

Well, yeah.

Me, Myself, and I

Moving on through the many things that we kick ourselves over, some parents ask: should Johnny have a sibling to draw him out? Or, should Johnny be an only child so that he can have my undivided attention? Families who have one kid may wonder if their little one is missing out, and parents of larger families may worry about being spread too thin. As with anything else, a kid on the autism spectrum is like any other kid, just more so. In our case, having both younger and older siblings seems to draw Grace out in different ways, and the kids really enjoy each other—except when they're trying to kill each other (well, they are siblings, after all).

Grace's older sister Lucy asks me a lot of questions about autism. In an unguarded moment, I told her that sometimes it feels like I have to reach around the autism to get to Grace. Lucy said, "Yeah, I know what you mean, Mommy. I really like her stories, but most of the time I feel like she is inside four walls of brick and I can walk around and around them but only she has the key to the secret doorway."

I'll let you in on a secret that you already know. You will, just as you did when you first became a parent, find a new normal. Your other family members shouldn't have to live in Autistic Spectrum World every minute of every day. The fact that Grace became a Big Sister during the year in which her sensory issues hit the fan turned out to be a blessing. In a perfect world, a perfect family might have decided that it was not the perfect time to add another sibling to the family, but we aren't perfect, and life doesn't work that way. And thank God! There is such a thing as paying too much attention to the problem and forgetting to see the child. Having younger siblings has drawn Grace out in ways that we could never have imagined, and Grace's relationships with her siblings are lovely, challenging, tumultuous, peaceful, happy, crazy, and sane.

How Come SHE Gets to Do That?

Like all parents, we have struggled with what we ought to expect of our children. This is yet another area in which a child on the autism spectrum is just like any other child, only more so. In our house, this is particularly noticeable when it comes to chores. The entire sequence of events is going to be different for kids on the spectrum, and the level of focus and intensity that you are willing to devote to getting the laundry done is going to fluctuate from day to day. It's easy to feel like you're failing when getting the dishwasher unloaded is either a solo effort or an exhausting tug-of-war. The truth is, all parents have to figure out how to balance being fair with realistically assessing the capabilities of their different kids. Maturity levels are going to be different, and past parenting experience may actually work against you.

> *I consistently lower her age in my mind by two years so I'm in sync with my expectations of her social behavior for her true age.*
>
> — J., CALIFORNIA

He is always bugging his younger brother, touching him, pulling him away from things, interrupts, teases, same negative behaviors over and over, doesn't seem to learn, very controlling.

— S., Oklahoma

LUCY'S TURN

SOMETIMES GRACE LIKES MY DOLLIES MORE
THAN SHE LIKES ME, AND MOM SAYS NOT TO TAKE
IT PERSONALLY. I STILL DON'T KNOW WHAT THAT MEANS.

No, *You're* a Doodoohead!

Then there's the sibling who enjoys tweaking Junior's sensitivities. There is a fine line between being sensitive toward a sibling's problem areas and having them run your life. Then again, you may find that your kids just act like siblings anyway. As observed by J. in Massachusetts:

Soft repetitive sounds bother him. His sister has a field day with that, as you can imagine. He can't seem to shut out background sounds.

Before you judge that sister too harshly, remember that she has an unusual burden as well, dealing with a sibling whose behavior makes no sense to her:

He's an absolute bully to them, insults them, hits them, destroys their things, tries to destroy their enjoyment of life, and is outright toxic to them. I've considered sending him to live with my mother in order to protect the other three from his nastiness. It is CONSTANT and nothing I've done has had any effect on his obnoxious, bullying behavior toward them.

Now that Lucy is eight, we do have conversations, initiated by her, that start with things like, "Mommy, does Grace do that because of her Asperger's?" She has also been known to ask me or Daddy, "Was that autistic?"

The Benefits of a Good Babysitter

Before you go into the fetal position and start crying (save that for the potty training chapter), the news is not all bad. Adults may "get" your child when other kids don't. One mom reported:

> *My child is rare and special and I can see he is unique. He is much more interesting than most other children. Adults love him!*

— A., CALIFORNIA

Once I got over the idea that all of my child's friends had to be children, life got a lot easier. Here I must sing the praises of Morgan, my son's godmother. Seemingly quite randomly, God sent us someone who has been endlessly compassionate about my children and their needs.

One day, after we had endured a particularly frustrating bout with pica, I came home to find that Morgan and Grace had made a cake, cut it into cubes, and piled it with dates and blueberries. Next to the cake was a sign that Morgan and Grace had made that said:

PRINCESSES DON'T:

eat snails
squish or kick people

PRINCESSES DO:

what their parents tell them to do
good things and are gentle
eat cake and dates

I'm Her Sister, Not Her Hostage

I'll give you a classic example of the mistakes we make/made and our newer approach to accommodating as much as we can without making the rest of the family feel like we're hostages in Autism World. (That concept, by the way, was one of the things that made my co-author think that this book is really important—helping people see that life goes on, it doesn't have to be all depressing, hard work—you just get on with enjoying life in new and different ways.)

I wound up taking Lucy, my oldest, to the circus on a Sunday evening. We had gotten discount tickets months and months in advance for the whole fam, before we really appreciated the fact that Grace would not really hang well with that much noise/stimulation. Well, she loves animals and well, you know, the tickets were Such a Deal! So off we went. Sure enough, I had to kind of drag her in (somewhat against my better judgment) and then once she hyper-focused on the show, she was fine. Until intermission. Once she broke focus, she wanted nothing more than to go home. We know from experience that if we force the issue on stuff like that, we're going to have a couple of days of her coming down off of that much stimulation. Frankly, half a circus is also plenty for a two-year-old. My older daughter, on the other hand, was more than ready for the second half. So I went online and found two last-minute tickets for the Sunday show; Ben stayed home with the others while Lucy and I went back and saw the whole thing. Everybody was happy. An effective, if expensive, way to make sure that nobody missed out because their needs conflicted with someone else's.

We live and we learn.

LUCY'S TURN

I GOT TO GO TO THE CIRCUS TWICE! EXCELLENT!

Paging Dr. Dolittle

Yes, the title of this chapter was "My Child and Other People" and, of course, animals are not people. We know that. Bobbi originally had this section as a separate chapter but I thought it went better here. Maybe I feel that way because animals can be a lot more comforting than people some days.

The relationship between animals and individuals with autism is the stuff of legend. The best book I've read on this subject is *Animals in Translation* by Temple Grandin. In addition to sharing some amazing insights about how autistic people think, Dr. Grandin shares amazing insights that help me to see that every "disability" has hidden gifts and that every gift has a cost. I laughed out loud when I read this one:

> *I used to take him to a local park where he would feed the ducks ... and he would chase them. I would always say, "You can't catch those ducks," and one day I turned around to see him sitting on the bench petting a duck that was sitting on his lap.*

> — L., Texas

I've heard that the perfect place for an autistic kid is a farm: animals, routine, the rhythm of the seasons, wide-open spaces, and limited conversation. Sometimes, I try to introduce a few farm-y elements into our suburban life. The cheapest therapy we ever got is our zoo membership. Grace happily rides the pony at the petting zoo until the cows, horses, and chimpanzees come home, and our zoo has a carousel too; it's like an Autism Spectrum double dip. Going around and around while on the back of either type of pony makes her think she's died and gone to heaven. Better yet, we go when the other kids are in school and the place is virtually empty. There is also something called equestrian therapy that you may want to try if it is available in your area. It is a wonderful, gentle thing. Someone Who Really Knows What He or She is Doing guides your child through caring for and riding a horse and magic happens.

Animals Aren't Exactly Gentle with Other Animals, Ya Know

Understanding that my child's senses and startle response have something in common with dogs and cows is more helpful than you might think. On the other hand, such knowledge can only go so far. I can't expect my daughter's lack of caution to go into remission when she is around her hairy, four-legged friends. Just because my child responds to animals doesn't mean that she IS an animal. Besides, animals bite one another too! Don't assume that because your kid is autistic that he's the horse whisperer. Animals will bite your kid if you don't teach her how to be safe around them. You may also see immature behavior around animals, especially unfamiliar ones.

As with everything else, painstaking repetition is the rule.

Use What You've Got

We frequently leverage our daughter's love of animals. We have been known to ask her, "Do you want this banana sliced or monkey style?" She always says monkey style, and we hand it to her in the peel. We also discuss in her presence how much the Three Bears love their porridge at times other than breakfast. Then, when we serve oatmeal to her, *voila!* She is (sometimes) willing to eat it because we've called it porridge. Never underestimate the power of a favorite plate or how much your child may love things that are gross. I am also not above a little bait and switch. I will offer a favorite food and then, when she goes for it, say brightly, "Of course you may have this as soon as you've had some yummy fruit! Now would you like an apple or some grapes??" In other words, the same kinds of things that you did with your other kids when they were very young, only more so and for a longer period of time.

I'm a big fan of equine-assisted therapy—maybe because I was one of those horse-crazy girls—so I'm happy Bobbi has gotten Grace involved. It seems like a good choice for her. We are fortunate to have a wonderful program (Spirit Horse) in our area that provides equine-assisted therapy for FREE to individuals with disabilities (I've heard of other facilities charging as much as $150 a session). Spirit Horse has also participated in research studies to determine if this type of therapy is helpful to children with ASD. The results have not been released yet, but I'm betting they found it very helpful.

On the not-so-good choice list for Grace—dolphin-assisted therapy. When I worked for a large school district in north Texas, we occasionally had children with ASD transfer into the district from California. A few of these had Behavior Intervention Plans (BIPs) that required the child to have dolphin-assisted therapy. Since we didn't have dolphins in our land-locked school district, we could never accept the child's BIP. While this angered the parents, it may have been a good thing. Cathy Williamson of the Whale and Dolphin Conservation Society reports that dolphin-assisted therapy is not only ineffective but may be dangerous to both the child and the dolphin (2008).

That said, as the owner of three dogs (including a therapy dog-in-training), I continue to be interested in the therapeutic use of animals for children with ASD. A meta-analysis conducted by Nimer and Lundahl (2007) found that animal-assisted therapy was effective in improving outcomes in four areas: autism-spectrum disorders, behavioral problems, emotional well-being, and medical difficulties. Dogs were the most commonly used animals and showed the most success.

We recently got Grace some fish, and she is having a whale of a time caring for them. It's going swimmingly. They're Betta fish; I'm glad that Dr. DeOrnellas warned me about the dolphins.

Special-Needs Sports and Activities

Here's an option that is so obvious, a lot of us have missed it. (I did, for a time.) In addition to friends and family, our support system can include activities designed for kids with special needs. Of course there is the Special Olympics, but what about the rest of the year? There are camping outings for families, classes for soccer, dance, ballet, art, music, swimming, photography, and many other activities. I had some initial resistance to trying this, but guess what? It was a chance for me to remember that my kid's activities are for *her*; they're not about me, or my hang-ups. When I sheepishly confessed to another mom how difficult it was for me to let go of the idea that my daughter could thrive in the class that was So Good for All the Other Kids, she smiled gently and said, "Yes, we call that the death of the dream."

Don't hesitate to try athletic and dance programs that are specially designed for kids with special needs. We have found these programs—and the families involved in them—to be wonderful. Grace is now signed up for Special Needs Creative Movement Class, and she has really embraced it. We'll be doing a lot more special-needs stuff. I've learned that *if you're going to worry about what "they" think, you can't win.* I hope you will make at least one special-needs program a part of your support system.

I've been surprised to learn that the resistance I referred to is not limited to me, but is shared by many other parents of kids with autism. Perhaps some parents don't want to put Tommy or Susie into a special-needs program because they hope that maybe they'll "grow out of it." Or maybe they're embarrassed by Johnny's lack of coordination.

But we all know that other people will judge us, or think it's our "fault" that our child has autism, and signing our child up for a

Special Needs program announces it to the judgmental world, putting our kids—and ourselves—at the mercy of the monumentally uninformed. The death of the dream? Oh, yes—but that would be Mommy's dream, not my child's dream. *She's* just fine! The hang-ups? *Those* would be mine.

Mothers Giving Diagnoses on Playgrounds: *Shut Up. Shut Up, Up, Up.*

As you've no doubt observed, people are going to notice—and comment upon—behaviors that are different. The things that might catch the attention of a preschool teacher or a stranger on a playground may include your child's avoidance of eye contact, spinning, or social immaturity.

> *K did not like eye contact. When she became verbal she would ask people to not look at her. At age 5 she would run the border of a fence to avoid eye contact with children who tried to talk to her.*
>
> — J., CALIFORNIA

Now might be a good time to reiterate: the behaviors that are most noticeable aren't generally that important. Then there are those folks who think that they're being helpful when they're really just butting in:

> *One lady told me he shouldn't have a sippy cup anymore. I felt irritated with her and haven't talked to her since. She was a little snotty about it.*
>
> *My mother-in-law told me I needed to spank him for discipline. That never worked. I considered that maybe I was too lax so I got very stringent on discipline which just made everyone more upset and unhappy. Then started not disciplining at all, which also didn't work for anyone.*
>
> — A., TEXAS

The most outrageous thing was at the grocery store several years back when someone said he needed his rear end beat. He was having a hard time and threw a fit and someone said that to me.

— J., OHIO

Speaking as a person who has been boundary-challenged from time to time, I can say emphatically that I am shocked by the lack of boundaries in today's world. That's a whole 'nother book (perhaps we can call it *People Who Need to be Slapped?*), and nobody has mistaken me for Miss Manners, but I'm just sayin'.

Whether it's the ignoramuses who tell you in the grocery store that People Like You Shouldn't Have Children and by the way, Control That Brat, or the mavens who diagnose your child at the soft play area at the mall, you are going to have to learn to deal with the way the world deals with your kid. You've probably already figured out that this isn't fun. Some days, I can handle intrusiveness with humor. Sometimes I have to use my Mom Look on them. Other days, I just want to be left alone. On any day, it's my job to protect my kid. That includes not allowing people to talk *about* her, *in front of her*, as if she's a potted plant.

Take a Card, Any Card

While we may have some level of understanding of our child's behavior, the rest of the world isn't likely to be kind. (Remember how clueless we used to be? Like last week.) Some parents actually carry around printed cards explaining that their child has a neurological disorder and they hand them to strangers who get a little too helpful or a little too cross when witnessing a meltdown, a hygienic challenge, or what have you. I know, I know, it sounds odd, but don't laugh. You may decide that handing someone a card is preferable to punching them in the face. (May I suggest offering a copy of this book instead?)

Maybe I'm overstating it a little, but I don't have to tell *you* what it feels like. I have been absolutely astonished at the high percentage of supermarket checkers who will slow down or stop what they are doing when I most desperately want to leave the store to say, "My, you have your hands full." I can't help noticing that this comment—which is also routinely made to my friends who have typical children, especially if they're melting down—is never, ever accompanied by an offer to help. Not that I'm bitter, but if I could just offer one word of advice to anyone who has ever even thought of using that phrase, here goes:

Shut.

Up.

Right now. What on *Earth* is someone supposed to say in response? If one does have one's hands full—which is often the case with small children anyway—it's not a welcome comment. On the other hand, if one is feeling particularly competent on a given morning and is told by a stranger, "My, but you have your hands full," it is especially deflating. The appropriate responses, in my opinion, range from a dead stare to "That's not a nice thing to say to anybody," to the ever-popular "Shut your face." My eight-year-old has said to me, right then and there, "Mommy, she is saying that because we are acting up, isn't she?" I love that kid.

Anyway, back to the cards. If you Google "autism information cards," you'll find the entire array, from apologetic to informational to the printed equivalent of a punch in the face. Come to think of it, maybe I need to print out a couple of those confrontational ones before I head to the grocery store.

WHAT I WISH I'D KNOWN

I HAVE NO OBLIGATION TO MAKE EYE CONTACT
WITH A STRANGER IN THE GROCERY STORE,
ESPECIALLY IF SHE IS TRYING TO CATCH MY EYE.

Wait'll Your Sister Hears about This

It's not just strangers, though. I also struggled with how much to tell Grace's siblings. It can be dangerous to improvise, as when your child asks what's wrong with Bubba anyway, or when Big Ears overhears you chatting with another adult. You should have an arsenal of one-liners ready for: "Mom, what's Asperger's? Mom? Oh, Mom? Can I have a cookie? What's autism? What's Asperger's? Can I have some Asperger's? Do I want some autism, Mom? Can I have a cookie now?" As the kids get older, the question becomes, "Is that because of autism?" We favor things like, "Because she's younger than you," or "Because she's older than you," or "There are things that you need too, and everyone is their own person." I also like, "She just doesn't feel like talking right now; you don't feel like talking sometimes too." As children get older, this isn't going to cut it, but you are going to be able to tell when additional information is going to be useful. You will need to trust yourself on this one.

I think it's important to stress how normal Grace's behavior can be because—let's face it—it's normal for *us*. Other people—whether they're family members or not—aren't going to have a relationship with a diagnosis, a label, or even the sometimes quirky behavior of your child; they are (or aren't) going to have a relationship with your child. As a parent, it's hard to resist the urge to try to cushion this truth. This is a tough line to walk. It gets worse than that, actually; as a parent, it's sometimes hard to get past the labels and the behavior to see our own kid. For me, this is sometimes very painful.

On my good days, when I am being the parent I want to be, I try to find a balance between being real with my kids *about what they already see* while still preserving some of their innocence and not burdening them. This is a tall order. With my oldest daughter, I have started to elaborate a little, along the lines of, "You know how Grace is really good at puzzles and doesn't like to play with friends as much as you do? She's her own person. Daddy and I are that way too sometimes, and it's called autism. It's just something that runs in our family." She will now ask me whether such-and-such is "because of autism," and then we talk about it. I have also cautioned Grace's siblings not to make *everything* about autism. In a recent interview with the *Wall Street Journal,* Temple Grandin addressed this topic. She said that when a young person talks to her about "my Asperger's" or "my autism," what she really wants to hear about is their interest in botany or astronomy or mathematics or music.

What I really need to show them is simple. I'm the one who makes it complicated. The truth is: Asperger's means that Grace doesn't have the words to tell us all that is inside her immense heart. It means that I sometimes have to be her voice when she can't express herself. It means that her brain is so powerful, it takes in too much for her to digest. Sometimes it means that the volume of life is just turned up a little too much for her. It means that she has an ability to concentrate that would put a genius to shame. It means that sometimes she seems a little younger and sometimes she needs to be alone more than you do. It means that she can feel the world turn, and so she spins to try to get into sync with it. It means that she's unique, just like you are.

I Have to Shut Up, Up, Up, Too

It's easy to pontificate about the nosy know-it-alls and how they Just Don't Get It, but I have to resist the urge to be one of those jerks sometimes. Of course, *I* only mean to enlighten and not to criticize, but I still manage (mostly) to keep my big mouth shut when I notice that four-year-old who melts down for no obvious reason, fusses about the snack, and won't play with the other kids or make eye contact. I surely have benefited from the gentle suggestions that have been made to me, I think. I don't want to be a buttinsky, honest. On the one hand, it's painful to see the parent suffering and treating the matter as a discipline problem. On the other hand, I could be wrong—maybe he is just an ungovernable terror.

REFERENCES:

Bauminger, N., & Kasari, C. (2000). Loneliness and friendship in high-functioning children with autism. *Child Development, 71*, 447-456.

Bauminger, N., Solomon, M., Aviezer, A., Heung, K., Brown, J., & Rogers, S. J. (2008). Friendship in high-functioning children with autism spectrum disorder: Mixed and non-mixed dyads. *Journal of Autism and Developmental Disorders, 38*, 1211-1229.

Nimer, J., & Lundahl, B. (2007). Animal-assisted therapy: A meta-analysis. *Anthrozoos, 20*, 225-236.

Williamson, C. (2008). Dolphin Assisted Therapy: Can swimming with dolphins be a suitable treatment? *Developmental Medicine & Child Neurology, 50*, 477.

CHAPTER TWELVE

Talk about It

We've been together for almost 200 pages now, and we've talked about everyone except you. The saying, "If Mama ain't happy, ain't nobody happy" was never more true than it is with our families. It's also true for good old Dad.

It was very liberating for me to realize that *this thing*, whatever you want to call it—ASD, Asperger's, an autism spectrum disorder, PDD-NOS, etc.—was bigger than me and I couldn't handle it alone. As you have probably already deduced, I did not come gently to this realization; I could not accept it without a fight. I am so determined not to be weak or let anyone down, and having a vulnerable child can send these tendencies into overdrive. So, let me try to help you avoid some of what I went through by just coming right out and telling you: you can't handle it alone, either. If you can, you need to come to my house and meet my kids and tell me what I'm doing wrong, *you big ol' liar, you*. For the parents who are raising these kids alone, or for those who are overwhelmed with the demands of job, home, and other kids, this goes double for you: *the hand that we have been dealt is not a one-person—or even a two-person—job.* Do not be ashamed or afraid to admit this. Some families work with a special preschool, an occupational therapist, their school district's services for children with special needs, or any other combination of competent, caring adults, but the reality is, we all need help.

WHAT I WISH I'D KNOWN

I WISH I HAD KNOWN HOW TO FIND AND ACCESS THE
AMAZING NETWORK OF OTHER PARENTS IN THE SAME BOAT.
EVERY CITY — AND MOST SMALL TOWNS — WILL HAVE
A SUPPORT NETWORK. REACH OUT. DO IT NOW.

I recently met a dad who is much further down this road than I am. He encouraged me to be open to sports activities geared towards kids with special needs. We have had many disasters (with a few great experiences mixed in, but, let's face it—mostly disasters) with swim lessons, ballet classes, and soccer clinics. This dad was especially enthusiastic about Special Olympics and what a blessing it has been in his family's life. It's been mortifying for me to realize the extent of my own resistance. This theme is echoed by author Julie Clark in *Asperger's in Pink,* in which she discusses her decision to put her daughter in a special-needs swim program. Her doubts were the same as mine: Does my kid really need this when her disability isn't physical? Is it going to make her (or is that *me*) feel weird? Are we taking a spot from a child whose special needs are greater? Are the other parents going to wonder why we're there? We've already had a belly full of not fitting in. As Julie Clark said in *Asperger's in Pink:*

> *One of the hardest things about raising a child with Asperger's is the feeling that our daughter has something invisible. We have often commented that life might be easier for her if there were some outward indicator.*

WHAT I WISH I'D KNOWN

WHEN ENOUGH WELL-MEANING PEOPLE IMPLY
THAT YOUR CHILD'S DISABILITY ISN'T REAL,
IT DOES GET INSIDE YOUR HEAD.

We needn't have worried. Our experience in special-needs equestrian therapy and ballet have been blessings that we would have missed if our lives had been different. In Ms. Clark's words:

> *There was such a sense of peace, of acceptance. For the first time, it felt as if our family truly belonged.*

— ASPERGER'S IN PINK, PAGE 170

She talks about the relief that she felt when she "set pride aside" and took advantage of the wonderful opportunities that are already there for our kids and our families.

Help! I've Fallen and I Can't Get Up

We were in treatment with Dr. DeOrnellas for more than a year when I observed, after a particularly rough patch with Grace, that one child with these issues takes the effort of three or four kids. Without hesitation, she observed that my number was too low. Understanding this made it much easier for me to accept help.

In our case, we have a strong, deep social network that includes other families with special needs. I am only human and I also have other children who don't need to spend their childhood in Autism Spectrum World 24/7. I am blessed to have an unusually supportive and involved husband who sees to it that I get mental health breaks, and he is very much on Grace's wavelength. I have devoted many pages to the beating that your child's ASD can give to your marriage, and I strongly recommend that you and your spouse/partner read this section together, especially if this is a challenging area for you. Better that you discuss it than ignore it, even if you argue about it. If you are doing this on your own—either as a single parent or as a parent with a spouse who isn't helping with the awesome responsibilities of your ASD kid—then take everything that I've said about needing help and multiply it times two, three, or whatever you need. *Never* let anyone make you feel like a wimp. This is just plain hard. I didn't say that you couldn't do this; I said that you can't to it *alone*. Nobody can.

Respite care is more important for us than it is for other parents. There, I've said it. I say: do what works. Here's a little quiz:

- Are you yelling at your kids all the time?
- Are you crying several times a week?
- Do you feel like your spouse isn't helping you enough?
- Are you exhausted and pissed off most of the time?
- Has it been too long since you've found your kids delightful?

If you answered yes to any of these questions, congratulations! You are honest. And more normal than you realize. You also need a break and some useful help. *Don't keep living that way. I am giving you permission to reach out for help, and I'm telling you that it doesn't make you weak or a bad parent.* You need to change things up a bit, which probably means that you need more help. More sleep probably wouldn't hurt either. An autism spectrum disorder isn't something that you "cure"; it is something that you manage, and it's not going to go away because of your superior efforts. You can't kiss this boo-boo enough times to make it all better, and truly, you don't need to. Remember the flight attendant who told you to first put on your own mask and then your child's while the plane is plummeting towards earth? Take that to heart. You aren't doing anyone any favors if you're stretched too thin. Don't beat yourself up for needing help and don't wait until you are at the end of your rope to ask for help. Mostly, what you probably need is a break.

Mommy Time

Some of you may be saying "Yeah, that sounds like a good idea, but I do not have Time For Me." It's really critical—I mean, absolutely sanity-saving—to make time for yourself. *Any* child can suck the soul out of you if you let her—that's just the nature of children—but our children do it with excellence. I don't care if you check into a motel for an afternoon to do nothing but sleep while your mom watches your kids. I don't care if you have to meet a friend at 7 a.m. on a Saturday to have breakfast while your spouse sleeps in with the kids; you have to get *completely away, physically,* from your child and your routine. I could totally relate to the parent who said:

> *The challenging thing is just finding the right time to have other relationships.*
>
> — J., OHIO

When we're not with our children, we're thinking about them every minute, or we're feeling guilty about NOT thinking about them every minute. Even if we can't shut that off, we have to at least hit "pause" and remember that we are human too. Otherwise, we may find ourselves melting down as often as our kids, and what good does that do anyone?

I, personally, suffer from delusions of adequacy. The idea that there is a boo-boo that I cannot kiss, a problem I can't solve, a need that I cannot meet with the sheer force of my will is simply baffling to me, but there you have it. It's okay. Of course this is bigger than we are. Duh. We need personal support systems, and we need some professional guidance, even if it's just a tune-up from time to time when things change and what used to work doesn't work anymore.

Take Off the Brass Bra

One of the surprises for me is how gut-wrenchingly hard it can be when things are going *well*. Yes, you read that right. When times really are tough, I can be a rock. It's later that I turn into a pile of Jell-o, burst into tears for no reason (or for really, really stupid reasons) and need extra sleep. This self-knowledge is really important; it helps me to let myself off the hook. There will be times when you need extra sleep, extra hugs, extra time away from the kids, and you shouldn't beat yourself up about it. I can't stress enough how important it is that you acknowledge your weak points and be unapologetic about pampering yourself. I'm not talking about self-pity; I'm talking about self-preservation. Life will take on a rhythm, no matter how weird things may seem right now. Being the parent of a child with special needs does *not* mean that you have to be a martyr. We do our kids no favors if we knock ourselves out trying to be Tireless Mommy all the time. That's not sustainable or necessary. As a matter of fact, I've figured out that it isn't even good for my kids. What am I setting them up for if I make them think that a woman has to run herself ragged all the time? What sort of resentments will I create in my other children if they see that I'm driving myself up a wall over their sister? I'm not doing them any favors if I can't show them how to live at peace in my own skin. This is my life, not a gauntlet or a quiz.

If you are tempted to skip this advice or can feel yourself starting to experience guilt at the thought of taking care of yourself, please stop and think about the following research study than came out in 2010. Quintero and McIntyre studied families with and without children with ASD. The mothers of the children with ASD reported more stress and depression than did the other mothers. Quintero and McIntyre found that the adjustment of the siblings of the children with ASD was significantly related to the well-being of their mothers. They found that siblings "are often exposed to increased parental expectations, decreased parental involvement, and increased respon-

> sibilities" (p. 38). When the mothers of children with ASD are stressed or depressed, the outcome for the typically developing children is compromised.
>
> So, if you don't feel that you can get help for yourself, do it for your other children.

It's Okay to Be Happy

Let's jump right into another sensitive topic. How about the guilt of enjoying how things are more peaceful when one of your kids isn't around? Maybe time is the best medicine for this one, because I promise that, if you give it enough time, this will be the case with different kids at different times. Get used to the guilt if you must, but take the breaks anyway.

You Like Her, You Really, Really Like Her!

One of the things that can send me right into the happy dance is when somebody "gets" my kid. When somebody "gets" your child, it can sometimes make you so happy you want to weep. Go ahead. I got a little drippy when I read this:

Many people are very encouraging—especially at church. One woman wept when she told me how my third son requested to be chosen during "Duck, duck, grey duck" at the end of the church year. Earlier that year he would have never voiced that he wanted to be chosen. It was sweet that she was also wrapped up in wanting to see him succeed!

— A., MINNESOTA

Conversely, I have learned to recognize that precious moment when a person's eyes roll back in his head when you mention the autism spectrum. These are the people who are as ignorant as I once was, and the thought bubble right above their head screams, "This parent is about to make an excuse for her horrible parenting and her terrible kid and I have to be polite and pretend I'm buying this crap!"

Later, when we had the diagnosis and I had done all the read-ing I could on the subject, I called a meeting with the principal and teachers to explain, as best as I could, what he had been dealing with and that he would need some extra help to get through the rest of high school. I was explaining the difficul-ties he has as best as I could and thought I had done a good job, when the science teacher who was head of the academic decathalon team said "you just described all the kids on my team." I was very frustrated with that statement, because while P had a lot of similar "geeky" behaviors, his were so extreme as to cause major problems in his life. I felt like this teacher had not taken anything I said seriously.

— L., Texas

When Your Mother-in-Law Thinks You're Just a Bad Parent

Some of you will also have to accept the sad fact that extended family is just not equipped to deal with this. Whether they are con-vinced that your child really is "normal" or they are freaked out and don't know how to relate to him, sometimes family just isn't going to know how to deal with Junior. I don't care how helpful a relative is; if the price of her help is that she's tearing you down and making you feel incompetent, that help is too expensive. We all have an obligation to draw a circle of protection around our families, and our kids are more vulnerable—and more easily mis-understood—than most. As I've said in other contexts, *do not take garbage from anyone. I don't care who they are.* Whatever "help" that may accompany the garbage is not, I repeat, *not* worth it.

I am among the blessed few who *don't* have this particular prob-lem—my in-laws are actually terrific—but I realize that this probably places me in the minority. As a matter of fact, one of my husband's family members responded to our disclosure of Grace's autism with, "Oh, I hoped you knew!" Some people have a child who eats light bulbs; others have mean in-laws. You don't get to pick your poison, but I am truly grateful for the support of our extended family. Just in case you think that this is the norm, take a listen to some moms in pain:

I have had to be very protective of him. Family has/had a hard time with this because all they knew of autism was Rain Man.

— S., OKLAHOMA

If I could tell the world one thing about him, I guess that I would tell them that there is a thoughtful, loyal, loving person hiding under that shell of inflexibility, hyper-emotionality, and know-it-allness that is looking for acceptance and love in return.

— R., ILLINOIS

WHAT I WISH I'D KNOWN

JUST BECAUSE MY CHILD HAS "SPECIAL NEEDS,"
THAT DOESN'T MEAN THAT I CAN'T HAVE ANY NEEDS AT ALL.

Maybe You'd Like a Play Date
with Someone Else

Ah, the dilemma. How do you talk to acquaintances without feeling that you're like the Queen of TMI (Too Much Information) or freaking them out? (Then there are the folks who think you're asking for them to tell you how to live your life when you're just trying to give some information, but that's a whole 'nother book.) How do you go to a new friend's house *without* warning them that your child may start getting aggressive, taking off his clothes, or stimming?

While I opted to write a book about it, I realize that's not for everybody. It's a delicate balance. How much information is too much information? How do you respect your child's privacy and give her an opportunity for people to encounter her without labels without putting her in unnecessarily difficult situations because the people around her aren't prepared? This is a tough one, and the answer is going to differ from person to person and from situation to situation, but I'll give you a hint. Remember when you went on that play date and Junior whacked the other child with a toy, melted down, did property damage, peed on your hostess' kitchen table, only wanted to ride on the spinny swing, and wouldn't acknowledge you when you spoke to him? That Other Mother called me, and she's steamed. I mean hopping mad. Not at Junior, because she doesn't know *what* made him act that way (okay, she just thinks he's an unmanageable brat), but at *you* because you failed to warn her. Sorry, but she asked me to tell you.

How can you make it up to That Other Mother? I can tell you my solution: when in doubt, I err on the side of over-disclosure or declining the social invitation. I figure that if people aren't comfortable with some basic information about what to expect and why, we shouldn't be hanging with them anyway. I try to recall the person that I was before kids. You know, the one who didn't want to see and hear Other People's Children in the restaurant, the one who wished that Other People's Children generally behaved better? While I am now oh-so-much more enlightened, sensitive, and tolerant about such things, I do still remember. When in doubt, I choose not to put Grace in a situation that is going to stress her out, and I also know that most other people have their own problems and just aren't going to want to deal with the extra challenges that we face. This can be lonely at first, but you will be pleasantly surprised at how many people will be kind, inclusive, and welcoming to you and your kids. This is especially true of the many folks who are faced with the same issues.

Nobody Puts Grace in a Corner ... Well, Okay, *She* Does

One of the major upsides of our situation is that we have the nicest people in our lives because *everyone else has fled.* Our world has become smaller—and that's okay. In the past, I made ridiculous excuses in response to perfectly lovely and reasonable invitations because I knew how things would play out if we just showed up and hoped for the best. As one mom put it, "Truth be told, our shrinking social circle is not due solely to people choosing not to choose us … but also our choice to avoid potentially stressful or emotionally draining situations." (*Asperger's in Pink*, Julie Clark, page 152). Our social life has changed a lot.

Fortunately, we now have more tools in our toolbox—not that there's no place for ridiculous excuses. My husband and I have become adept at tag-teaming, and we do have some fearless babysitters. (Thanks, Laura, Alexandra, and Morgan. We love you!) We also have friends who know our limitations and who aren't offended if we say no, offer to host, or ask if we can show up for half of a party. Familiarity is also a huge help; after a time, most of the people that you are going to encounter are either going to be familiar with your situation or they don't want to be burdened with the details.

Really, it's actually good. Generally, she'd rather be at home anyway. Life is too short to spend worrying about when the time bomb of non-disclosure is going to detonate in your face, or when your child is going to be in over his head. Not coincidentally, you may find that the people who are comfortable with your child are true friends to you. I'm not talking about tennis friends (and I have nothing against tennis); I'm talking about friends with whom you can cry until you throw up. Sometimes, knowing that you have those friends if you need them takes away some of the need to cry, in which case I am strongly in favor of playing tennis with them.

It's also important to have realistic expectations of people. Folks will let you down, and you can't let it poison all your relationships. No matter how much someone else may care, it isn't her job to make it all better. She may be your sister, she may be your neighbor, but she may also be profoundly uncomfortable with your child and his differences. And she may not be good at letting you know. Not everyone is going to be comfortable communicating with clarity and maturity. I probably err on the side of not wanting to burden another parent, not because I'm a hero but because I've been, as they say, snakebit. Allow me to relate a small example of what I mean: I once had another mom offer to watch Grace for a brief amount of time; it was a pretty unprecedented thing for me, and I felt that I'd laid the groundwork properly—spent months doing it, actually, and confirmed that very morning. She just—whoops!— wasn't home when I showed up to drop my daughter off. I can warn you about this kind of thing, but I can't make it any easier for you. It's a heartbreaker. The worst part of that situation was trying to console Grace. It was just awful. Don't let experiences like this make you bitter. The truth is, our kids are a challenge, and not everyone is going to want to join us in this journey. It turns out that our children aren't the only ones with communication problems. Many people have trouble saying no when what they mean is "Hell, NO." Embrace the ones who accept you and your child.

He Loves Me, He Loves Me Not

It's not just other people who don't give you the warm fuzzies about your child's behavior. One of the challenges of raising a kid like ours is the lack of feedback from the child himself. Part of what hurts so bad is the fact that it ain't exactly easy to feel warm and fuzzy all the time towards a kiddo who is:

a) not relating to us;
and
b) driving us nuts.

I am here to absolve you of your guilt. Of course, you love your child. (Come on, now. You wouldn't have read this far if you weren't passionately concerned about him.) As with any other issues, navigating the emotional ties with our kids entails new rules that neither we nor our child have on board as standard equipment. As one mom put it,

I remember praying that I would have the same affection for M that I did for other kids. Of course, I would jump in front of a bus for her, but she was so independent, so reserved. It

was noticeable to the extended family as well. Why was I rais-ing such a cold child?

— S., TEXAS

This sentiment was echoed over and over by parents in one form or another:

The hardest thing about life with my son is trying to reach him emotionally. I love him so much ... yet I don't think he can really feel emotion the way most people do. I guess the reverse is the most challenging for him. He does not under-stand why some things he says or does hurt people's feelings. He does not seem to understand why "not caring" about peo-ple's feelings is any big deal.

— L., TEXAS

Unless and until you have a child on the autism spectrum, you may not realize how important it is to get warm fuzzies from the kiddo. Another shocker is the realization of how much you, as a parent, may enjoy the adoration of others that is directed towards your adorable child. As much as we'd all like to think that we Don't Care What Others Think, it hurts when a stranger sees your child acting out and tells you that people like you shouldn't have chil-dren (yes, a mom actually related that one to me). It is also a natural high for a parent to see how people delight in oohs and ahhhs of grandparents, librarians, and the random stranger at the mall. All that I can say is that it's character-building to get over this. Don't let it kill your buzz, I say.

What Happened to My Marriage?

We've already talked about the challenge of enlisting the involve-ment of your other children without ruining their lives. We've talked about how your child's autism will alter your relationships with the rest of the world. Now, we're going to get even more per-sonal. We're going to talk about your marriage. Some of you have already parted ways with your spouse, but you may want to read this section anyway. A child with special needs can be a strain on any relationship, not just the intimate ones. I appreciated the honesty of the parents who wrote:

My husband's response was not good! He still struggles with it, because he has an image in his head of what his son is and P can never be that person. He still, occasionally, does not believe that Asperger's exists, and thinks his son is just worthless. Later he feels guilty for expressing that to me. He never says it to P, but I know that P feels it.

— L., TEXAS

K's behavior causes a lot of stress on the marriage ... I'm generally seen as the over-reactive one. I feel my husband was either in denial or is uncomfortable to agree with me. He'd rather I take responsibility to explore or to acknowledge K has patterns that don't fall in the norm.

— J., CALIFORNIA

Sadly, I could give you pages of stories like this. I once met the father of a teenager with autism. He told me that the support group that formed when his child was a preschooler had disbanded because he and his wife were the only intact couple left. In *Louder than Words,* Jenny McCarthy pulls no punches about marriage—and divorce. She discusses the statistics and is very candid about the end of her marriage. I don't have to tell you that parenting an autistic child can be a grenade dropped right in the middle of your marriage; one parent can overreact and one underreact (or perceive one another to be doing so). If one spouse is convinced that your child needs some help, the whole family is going to be involved, one way or the other. Better that it should be done cooperatively and positively.

I Could Be Wrong, but the Following Is Worth Considering

I won't sugar-coat this. It's very difficult to deal with the fact that your spouse doesn't "get" something that is so painful, so challenging, and so hard to face alone.

If your spouse seems to be withdrawing, not contributing, and generally blowing off the challenges you are having with your child, consider that perhaps he or she really does care and is on the autism spectrum him/herself. Perhaps the things that are driving you up a wall seem absolutely normal to your spouse. The same compassionate strategies that work in dealing with your child might just work in dealing with your spouse—or yourself.

WHAT I WISH I'D KNOWN

I WISH I HAD UNDERSTOOD EARLIER JUST HOW VERY,
VERY ASPIE BOTH OF US CAN SOMETIMES BE.
IT COULD HAVE SHED LIGHT ON SOME NEEDLESS AREAS
OF CONFLICT. IT IS ALSO A RELIEF TO LOOK AT MY CHILD
SOMETIMES AND SAY, "HONEY, YOU AREN'T ALONE;
MOMMY LIKES TO LISTEN TO THE SAME SONG
NINETEEN TIMES IN A ROW TOO."

It Can Be Done

So, now that I've convinced you that marital strife and breakdown is the norm in families like ours, let me give you some good news. Some of us really are happily married. At the risk of sounding presumptuous, let me assure you that we have learned much by trial and error, and I will share a bit (knock on wood) of what works and doesn't work for us.

Daddy's Turn

Like all couples, my husband and I are not clones. Even though we are greatly in sync on parenting issues, having an ASD kid will test you to your limits and beyond. One of the things that I have learned over the years is that Ben is more on Grace's wavelength than anyone else is, including me. When the two of them have time alone together, she is generally better behaved and calmer afterwards. Here was The Big Lesson for me: It is Not My Job to play cruise director with them. Quite often, they go to the park or just sit together and do nothing. They are as happy as two peas in a pod.

BEN SAYS

I ESPECIALLY LIKE IT WHEN SHE WANTS TO SWING FOR HOURS WHILE I WATCH THE LAKE.

Who am I to criticize? It's working. Ladies, if you are tired of wondering when your husband is going to spend Quality Time with your kid, you may be pleasantly surprised to realize that the time that they spend together while she's counting her fingers, rearranging her shell collection, or playing with Mr. Potato Head while he's on his laptop really does count. For the two of them, it may be just what they need.

He's a Homebody; I'm Not

One of our biggest challenges—and I will confess that this is a strong point for my husband and a weak point for me—is to avoid taking on too much. You probably won't be surprised to learn how well he focuses and how he is, unlike me, quite content to do just one thing at a time. Quite often, that is our saving grace. We frequently fall back on our Don't Try To Do More Than One Thing Per Day Rule, especially where the kids are involved. If you are at your wit's end, my first piece of advice—I mean, my very first—

would be the following: for the next month, say a big fat NO to everyone and everything except yourself and your immediate family. You may be pleasantly surprised—nay, shocked!—at the results of this one change.

BEN SAYS

YOU'VE REALLY SUFFERED OVER THIS. TO ME, IT WAS
NO BOTHER AT ALL. I LIKE BEING AT HOME WITH YOU!

Remember the story about Patrick Henry telling the other Revolutionary War dudes that they could all hang together or they would certainly hang separately? It totally applies here. As with any other aspect of parenting, a team approach limits the child's ability to divide and conquer. In our case, we have come up with a code word for those moments when the marital radar may not be at its height. Either of us is able to, by saying this word, communicate to the other:

We!

Must!

Leave!

Now!

The launch sequence has begun.

It is also important for spouses to be very clear on who is better at what. In my house, for example, Ben is able to get inside Grace's head much better than I can (gee, I wonder why that is?). I could respect that, or I could resent it. Smart woman that I am, on my good days, I respect it. Sometimes it's Mom who takes the lead; sometimes, it's Dad. Our situation is a bit like that of A. in Texas, which is to say, a little of both:

My husband has more patience than I do, is less of a disciplinarian than me. He has some Aspie in him so he's very good at relating to my son on his level with technical type stuff and things both he and my son find interesting that I have no understanding of. I do almost all of the research and have spent MANY hours researching. My husband just helps me implement what I decide we need to do.

If the statistics are any indication, having a child with an ASD will, in short order, make you much more married than you ever dreamed possible or not married to each other at all. You can have a good marriage; I am living proof. I say that with humility, sort of like this person:

It almost drove us apart for a long time, but we both saw how difficult his life would be if we didn't do our very best to help him. With that, we both committed ourselves to the happiness and welfare of our son. We are totally bonded to him and he is to us. He's made our relationship stronger. We've had to re-do totally our way of doing things and it hasn't been easy, but it works.

— J., Ohio

I can't stress too much the importance of nurturing yourself and your marriage relationship. The children I have seen be most successful are the ones that have healthy parents and whose parents provide a united front. Don't feel guilty about taking time for yourself. As Bobbi said, if you don't put on your own oxygen mask first, you can't breathe—physically or emotionally—and you can't help your child.

The same can be said for your marriage. Take care of it first. The best thing we can do for our children is to show them what a good relationship looks like. It forms the basis for all of their future relationships. I often "prescribe" that couples reinstate date nights. Most couples I see haven't been out together without the kids in years. What used to surprise me is the resistance that I get. Now I realize that many couples are not comfortable spending time together without the kids to act as a buffer. Don't let that happen to you. Take turns planning an evening out. I recommend once a week but if that isn't possible, don't settle for less than once a month. Your partner should be your best friend and your greatest support.

REFERENCE:

Quintero, N., & McIntyre, L. L. (2010). Sibling adjustment and maternal well-being: An examination of families with and without a child with an autism spectrum disorder. *Focus on Autism and Other Developmental Disabilities, 25*(1), 37-46.

CHAPTER THIRTEEN

There Is No Finish Line

So, now that I've convinced you that you and every member of your family are on the autism spectrum, where do you go from here? Hopefully you've started to realize that life is going to be a little different than you'd planned, and that you can survive and even thrive. Hopefully you are pointed in the right direction to find the help you'll need. So, now what? Even under the best of circumstances, we parents are prone to project endlessly about our kids' future challenges. One mom in Oklahoma summed up some common fears about our special kiddos:

> *I hope he can make friends and marry some day. I hope he will learn how to be selfless and gain empathy for others. My greatest fear is that he won't know God and know the peace that comes from knowing him. He is very concrete and God is hard for him to understand.*

Relationships in general, including relationships with God, were a common theme with the parents we surveyed. Temple Grandin discusses the religion issue in several of her books. She acknowledges and confronts the common belief that individuals with autism *can't* believe in a higher power because of the way that their brains are wired. She asserts, convincingly, that love of repetition and routine can apply to things like prayers, church attendance, and religious practices, and she says that this has been a positive thing for her. We want our kids to have a quality of life, and the things that most of us find central to the quality of our lives are not necessarily as important to our kids—relationships and spiritual connections happen to be prime examples.

> *The hardest part is that it is exhausting and there is a fear that K will not know a healthy relationship or peace and happiness.*
>
> — J., CALIFORNIA

You need to keep in mind that you're not always going to reach a solution—at least, not right away. Experience, training, and reading are all tools in our arsenal. We have to keep educating ourselves. When I asked L. in Texas what tool she wished she'd had earlier on, she replied:

> *Just more info. You can't read enough. I think you have to constantly drill into yourself, this is a neurological disorder and your child needs the tools to help him deal with this situation. You are not a doctor and you don't have all the answers. Get help when you need it. You have to be able to pull the emotion out of situations because it really is not about emotion, it is about a particular situation that your child hasn't figured out yet, and you are the only one who can make sure he gets the proper tools.*

Sometimes I have to remind myself that our kids won't always be small. Those of us who have kids with developmental delays are going to have—how do I say this gently?—older, larger toddlers to contend with. These days, when we want to see folks, we either encourage them to visit us in our home, we do short, controlled visits to familiar places, or we leave the kids with our sitter. If my kids want to wear what my dad used to call "outlandish costumes," I don't make a fuss. I figure that if my child's attire is generally appropriate for the climate and doesn't attract the (negative) attention of the authorities, I'm not going to make a big deal.

The Song That Never Ends

There is nothing like recovery. He will be like this his whole life.

— A., TEXAS

The unexpected blessing is that I no longer assume I may judge any family's choices. People need more support, less judgment, and that is no matter what their situation ... it's all relative and it's all about relationships. The first relationship I learned to look at was with myself. I can accept my differences with more compassion too.

— J., CALIFORNIA

Life for me became much easier once I realized that there was no amount of interaction, therapy, reading, prayer, support, or *whatever* that was going to change the fundamental chemistry of my beautiful child's brain and central nervous system. *This was a life-changing realization.* She lives in a world where the volume is turned up too loud, her emotions hit her like a tsunami, and people's responses often don't make sense to her. There is much that I can and should do as her mom. Learning to cope and work around the extra challenges is a huge task for her and for us. We are helping her to learn to mediate the world. That's not the same as thinking that there is something here to "fix" or driving myself nuts trying to do it. It also helps to accept the reality and not to see it as an indictment of us or our families. This may take time. I have an acquaintance who refuses to explore whether her child is, in her words, "The A Word." While I sympathize with the pain and the fear behind this approach, it's not what a child needs, especially if that child could benefit from some understanding, some appropriate therapy, and some accommodations. Yes, it's hard to be the parent of a child with autism. My child is who she is, whether I have a label on her or not. The question is: do I accept her? In *Louder than Words,* the mom of an autistic son is gently told by the diagnosing doctor that her son is the same kid he was before they walked into the doctor's office.

> *I don't see this diagnosis as a burden, rather a guideline to know what things need to be done and how to get there.*
>
> — R., Illinois

I have to be willing to understand my daughter because the rest of the world isn't going to stop and explain itself to her. Our kids need us to help them, and we can't even begin to help them until we have some clue about what the world looks like to them. Since my daughter is high-functioning, the paradox is that, on the good days, she almost "passes" for typical. This makes the inevitable differences seem even harder for people to understand without blaming the parent.

For your convenience, I include here a "Letter To Whom It May Concern" that I encourage you to use as you see fit (perhaps you'll use better judgment than I do and omit the first two paragraphs):

Dear *[don't put what you want to put here,*
like Hard-Core Old-School Disbeliever/Teacher/
Neighbor/Mother-in-Law/Jackass, etc.]:

You've mentioned to me once or twice that you think Junior is a little different. Actually, you've intimated that he's a psycho and I must be a really, really, really bad parent. I've spent some time in the fetal position as a result of your snottiness, but this isn't about me; it's about you. I was once an uninformed jerk like you, and I'm hoping that you mean well and just don't know any better.

Perhaps I can't dissuade you from your belief that all that my child and I need is a good whack in the rear, but I'm going to try. Judge me if you must, but first tell me this: when was the last time that your child tried to peel the skin from her arms (repeatedly) with a potato peeler? (And no, toddlers don't count.) Now, for the bonus round: how would that make YOU feel? On second thought, I'm not really mad at you. I'm just tired of trying to make you understand, so I'm going to let a total stranger (a couple of them, actually) take a crack at your hard, hard head.

Please accept this copy of *What I Wish I'd Known about Raising a Child with Autism*, with my compliments.

Judge me if you must, but please give it a read.

Love and Kisses,

[YOUR NAME HERE]

Much of our happiness or misery in life comes from how we've set our expectations. You may be wondering what to expect in adolescence and beyond. It's important to remember how much we have in common with *all* parents when it comes to worries and unknowns. Yes, your experience will be different than you expected, but you've already started figuring that out. You will acquire the skills that you need. More good resources are available every day. The point of this book is not to convince you that you can't handle this; it's to assure you that you can't handle this alone. *Nobody can.* It's okay. Hopefully by now you know that you're not alone.

Now What?

Now what, indeed. That'll be the title of our next book.

Actually, when I am tempted to worry too much about the future, I read *The Way I See It* and *Developing Talents,* both by Temple Grandin (or, as she is known to me and my husband, The Authority). In both books, Dr. Grandin makes a strong case for not letting your child's limitations define him. Autism entails both disability and giftedness, if we must use labels. Is your kid uncomfortable in social situations? Yes, you need to be sensitive, but you also will need to push him out of his comfort zone over time. There are all sorts of people—both professionals and other parents—who can help you to figure out how. What works for someone else may or may not work for your kid. You don't have to figure this out all by yourself.

Lest You Get the Wrong Idea ...

I want to assure you that the challenges continue and that I am a fellow traveler, working to be an Ordinarily Good Parent. When we think we're in control, that's when we need to start to worry. That's probably true for all parents anyway.

Allow me to illustrate.

Shortly before Grace's fifth birthday, when I thought that I was done writing this book, I had a day that would have laid me flat even a year before. I do not exaggerate when I say that Grace's behavior was unprecedentedly, amazingly bad, and all at once.

It was our anniversary, and my husband had given me a dozen roses. Grace *ate* them! Okay, she didn't eat the whole dozen; I managed to stop her after she had eaten only two of them. But that was just the beginning. In addition to eating two of the roses, Grace also twice dumped the petals that her sisters and I had gathered up. Let me sum it up by saying that Grace has been compelled to personally apologize to each member of our family, and that a professional carpet cleaning was immediately scheduled.

Midway through this day, I had an epiphany of sorts as I took a look at the linen closet that she had emptied onto the floor (hey, at least it didn't involve scissors this time). I realized, to my amazement, that *I wasn't upset.* I wasn't thrilled, but my emotions were more in the shrug zone than the hair-on-fire zone. Feeling very Clint Eastwood, I narrowed my eyes at my daughter and said, "Remember when I cried the first time you did this?"
Lessons learned:

- Parent the child, not the mess. When my child is in Octopus Mode—that is, when she seems to grow multiple extra limbs—as I am trying to clean up the first mess and she has moved on to the third, I must focus on *her*. We can grow some more roses and replace the broken dishes, but we can't lose sight of the long-term goal to help her control her behavior. While there may be exceptions for things like broken glass, it is really more important to help my child learn to control herself and find out how she needs to be directed—or if she just needs to be held.

- If we do more than one activity with her that is outside the home and around people in a day, we are going to pay the price for a couple of days afterward. The day before the rose fiasco, my husband and I spoke about the fact that we knew that we were in for a doozy because we had dared to bring her to church *and* her sister's Peter Pan performance all in one weekend.

- I am strong. I now take in stride situations that would have had me in the floor like a pile of pudding a couple of years ago—and I used to be an Assistant DA. This knowledge, as well as my ability to stop caring what others think of me or my parenting, is mostly a gift from Grace.

- If I had to choose, I guess it's better that my child, and not my husband, was the one to bite the heads off my roses.

Last year, we had a Ph.D. student perform an assessment of Grace for the purpose of setting goals for her equestrian therapy program (honestly, I don't know who's more excited about the horses, me or Grace). Jennifer, the lovely, talented future Ph.D., made the most encouraging comment. She told me that we reminded her of another family she had worked with, whose kid was very high-functioning. When Jennifer positively commented to the parents about how good their son's behavior was, one of parents said something along the lines of, "Yes, but if we removed all our accommodations for one week and called you back for another assessment, I think you'd see how he *really* functions without our support system."

I can't think of a lovelier, more encouraging thing that she could have said to us. It felt incredible to have someone recognize and validate—even in this indirect way—the efforts and progress we were making as a family. Jennifer's comment made us feel like we were doing something *right*. Sometimes, when we're in the thick of the treatments, schedules, and accommodations, it is easy to forget that those everyday efforts are forming a foundation on which our Grace can stand. Like all of us, she will grow up and take her place in the world. Our task is to help her to make it, to find it, to fight for it. Yes, we may bring gluten and dairy in and out of our diets, and yes, we may make as many mistakes and omissions as the next family, but we are doing our best and our best is what our daughter needs. Please, please believe that your best is what your child needs. He doesn't need the Perfect Program, the Perfect Therapist, or the Perfect Anything. He needs love; he needs you.

Afterword

Let me be clear. I don't want people to think that this is easy or that we have it knocked. As often as not, we feel more like the bug than the windshield. This is not fun to deal with, and it is no joke. My sense of humor often saves my sanity, and I love my husband and kids. I would not trade them. And yes, there are a million blessings that go along with autism. I am also gratified and humbled by the idea that we might be an encouragement to other families dealing with various forms of autism. Our personal growth, self-awareness, maturity, parenting skills, you name it ... there have been blessings to go with every difficulty. Grace is happy and well. Nonetheless, of course I wish that things could be different for my baby. I wish that things weren't so hard for her. I wish that she didn't have to struggle the way that she does with things that aren't painful or difficult for me. I wish that I could bear more of the difficulty for her.

What does Grace think of all this? I asked her, "How would you like it if I put you in a book?"

Remember, she is a very literal thinker. She looked perplexed, and I realized that she was trying to figure out how she'd squeeze between the front cover and the back cover.

"Let me try that again," I said. "Do you know that I wrote a book about you? Is that good?"

She smiled and said, "Oh, yes, Mommy. Can you make me famous and put me in a movie?"

"Well, that is unlikely," I admitted. Grace replied, "Then can I have a cupcake?"

Bobbi's Annotated Bibliography

Yes, I am one of those dorks who thinks that I know about something because I've read a book about it (or, for that matter, written one). While parenting my children—all of them—has done much to disabuse me of *that* notion, I am an avid reader and old habits die hard. Here are some resources that I found useful. If you know of other books that should be in future bibliographies, I'd love to read them, so let me know about them.

Let's Start at the Very Beginning, a Very Good Place to Start

If I could hand-pick the next books you are going to read, it would be the books listed in this section. They would be a good "starter kit," depending on their relevancy to your particular circumstances:

Ten Things Every Child with Autism Wishes You Knew
by Ellen Notbohm, Future Horizons 2005,
ISBN: 9781932565300.

As good a starting point as you're going to find. I love this writer's style, and I didn't feel like an idiot, even though she pointed out things that, upon reflection, should have been obvious to me.

Raindrops on Roman by Elizabeth Burton Scott, M.A., Robert Reed Publishers 2009, ISBN: 9781934759240

If you've already gotten confirmation that your child has autism, you may be wondering what to do next. Elizabeth Scott has written two books that could be a great help to you. In her memoir *Raindrops on Roman*, she introduces the reader to her son, Roman, and makes a compelling case for the importance of hands-on, loving parenting as an agent of healing. Her next book goes into more detailed, practical applications of that love (*Skills and Drills*, below).

Autism Recovery Manual of Skills and Drills: A Preschool and Kindergarten Education Guide for Parents, Teachers, and Therapists by Elizabeth Burton Scott, M.A. and Lynne Gillis, O.T., Robert Reed Publishers 2010, ISBN: 9781934759387.

Skills and Drills is a valuable tool kit, especially for a first-time parent. She gives detailed, common-sense suggestions and instructions, and *Skills and Drills* is co-authored by an occupational therapist. Mrs. Scott's approach is very compatible with my philosophy: Drop everything! Hug your kids! Play with them! Give them real toys! Give yourself a break and don't forget to pray! Do not allow them to lose themselves in television and electronic games! While this is good advice for any parent, it is absolutely crucial for the parent of a child with autism. We don't just bring our children into the world on the day they're born; it's a process, and this is especially true for a child on the autism spectrum. Every day is a day that can be spent bringing your child into our world and helping him learn to function in it. We cannot squander the gift of a day, especially when our children are young and developing rapidly.

Asperger's Syndrome: A Guide for Parents and Professionals
by Tony Attwood, Ph.D., Jessica Kingsley Publishers 1998,
ISBN: 9781853025778.

This book is an excellent encyclopedia of what you will need to know
and is a great starting point.

*Home Educating Our Autistic Spectrum Children: Paths Are
Made By Walking* by Kitt Cowlishaw and Terri Dowty,
Jessica Kingsley Publishers 2002, ISBN: 9781843100379.

I know, I know, I should put this in the education section. I just
can't, because this book really is about life. Even if homeschooling
is the last thing you'd ever consider, you should read this collection
of essays by a baker's dozen parents. These parents moved me to
tears with the unvarnished truth about themselves, their kids, and
their interactions with teachers, doctors, and psychologists. I found
it to be a welcome "reality check" about what I might expect from
thirteen families who have been farther down this road than I have.

The Curious Incident of the Dog in the Night-Time
by Mark Haddon, Vintage 2004, ISBN: 9781400032716.

This book blew my mind. Yes, it's fiction, but it's an amazing peek
into the mind of an autistic teenager. "Well written" seems too mea-
ger of a compliment. You will never view your child's behaviors in
the same way once you've read this book.

*The Out-of-Sync Child: Recognizing and Coping with Sensory
Processing Disorder* by Carol Kranowitz, Perigee 2006,
ISBN: 9780399531651.

This was one of the first books I read when I was putting the pieces
of the puzzle together. Once I understood that sensory issues were
real and often related to autism spectrum disorders, my education
had begun in earnest, so I owe this author a debt of gratitude.

For the Kids

These books explain autism issues on a child's level and could be read by or with a child as young as six years old:

Rescued by a Cow and a Squeeze: Temple Grandin
by Mary Carpenter, PublishAmerica 2003,
ISBN: 9781591298809.

Asperger's, Huh? By Rosina Schnurr, Ph.D.
(Illustrated by John Strachan), Anisor Publishing 1999,
ISBN: 9780968447307.

May I also recommend to you anything ever written by Cheri Meiners, whose website is www.freespirit.com/catalog/author_detail.cfm?
AUTHOR_ID=109. Her books, with titles like *Share and Take Turns* and *Join in and Play*, are wonderful.

These aren't books, but we love the videos from Model Me Kids (*Modelmekids.com*) too. Need to prepare your child for a play date? Try "Time for a Play date." We watched "I Can Do It!" to prepare for a birthday party, and it was amazing to see the skills and confidence that my daughter gained.

Autism and Girls

Asperger's and Girls by Tony Attwood, Ph.D., Temple Grandin, et al., Future Horizons 2006, ISBN: 9781932565409.

This is a series of essays by professionals, young women with Asperger's, and their family members. The information about the unique vulnerabilities of adolescent girls in social situations (mean girls are just the start; wait till your daughter starts to date) is invaluable.

Asperger's in Pink by Julie Clark, Future Horizons 2010,
ISBN: 9781935274100.

This first-hand story of one parent's struggle with discovery, disclosure, and understanding of her daughter's ASD will be especially
encouraging—and enlightening—to those of you whose kids are
so high-functioning that teachers and extended family sometimes
just think that you're a bad parent. As the author says, "Simply
put, some people still think we're full of it." You may want to save
this one for a truly rainy day when nobody "gets" you or your
child. This book is also a helpful discussion of the unique challenges presented by girls on the autism spectrum and a survey of
one mom's odyssey with her child's school system—you'll hear it
all, from the sublime to the ridiculous, with a few people in the
middle who just need to be slapped.

When You Need Laughter—and Insight

Keep these books on hand for those days when you feel like rocking in a corner and sucking your thumb. Curl up with one of these
books and laugh until you make embarrassing noises instead. It's
helpful sometimes to realize that you're not alone and that you
really can see humor in every situation.

*Laughing and Loving with Autism: A Collection of "Real Life"
Warm and Humorous Stories* by R. Wayne Gilpin,
Future Horizons 1993, ISBN: 9781885477040.

More Laughing and Loving with Autism by R. Wayne Gilpin,
Future Horizons 1994, ISBN: 9781885477125.

Much More Laughing and Loving with Autism
by R. Wayne Gilpin, Future Horizons 2002,
ISBN: 9781885477781.

My Altar before Temple Grandin

Yes, Dr. Grandin rates her own section in my bibliography. This amazing woman, who teaches animal science at the university level, writes bestsellers, and is personally responsible for making America's handling of livestock more humane, is autistic. Before she came along, autistic people didn't have a voice, and neither did cows. If you have never heard of her, drop my book right now and read everything she's ever written.

Animals in Translation: Using the Mysteries of Autism to Decode Animal Behavior by Temple Grandin, Ph.D. and Catherine Johnson, Scribner 2004, ISBN: 978-0743247696.

Is Dr. Grandin using autism to explain animal behavior, or is it the other way around? Either way, this book is unique, unforgettable, and brilliant.

Developing Talents: Careers for Individuals with Asperger's Syndrome and High Functioning Autism by Temple Grandin, Ph.D. and Kate Duffy, Autism Asperger's Publishing Company 2008, ISBN: 9781934575284.

This book discusses a variety of careers that may be just right for folks on the autism spectrum and explains why. Some of them may surprise you.

Emergence: Labeled Autistic by Temple Grandin, Ph.D. with Margaret M. Scariano, Warner Books 1996, ISBN: 9780446671828.

Temple Grandin's amazing personal story. She has overcome impossible odds and brought hope to untold thousands of families.

The Way I See It: A Personal Look at Autism and Asperger's by Temple Grandin, Ph.D., Future Horizons 2011, ISBN: 9781935274216.

A compilation of articles that Dr. Grandin wrote for *Autism Asperger's Digest* magazine. It builds on her earlier books and covers new ground.

Thinking in Pictures and Other Reports from My Life with Autism by Temple Grandin, Ph.D., Vintage 2010, ISBN: 9780307739582.

Once I read this book, I had a much better understanding of how my kid thinks. Yes, every person is different and every case of autism is unique, but the general way of thinking that is natural to me is *not* natural to my child. This book brought me into her world and helped me to understand how to speak her language.

Unwritten Rules of Social Relationships by Temple Grandin, Ph.D. and Sean Barron, Future Horizons 1995, ISBN: 9781932565065.

My husband loves this book. He especially loved the rule: "Not everyone who is nice to you is your friend." If you have an autism spectrum disorder, or if you have a child or co-worker who does, this book will explain, in detail, where the social pitfalls are and how costly miscommunication can be.

This section would not be complete without a HUGE recommendation that you watch the video of the 2010 HBO movie *Temple Grandin*, starring Claire Danes. Not only did it enlighten me, it made my mascara run, big-time.

Educating Your Child

Whether you homeschool or not, these books are full of good ideas.

Teaching Montessori in the Home: Preschool Years
by Elizabeth G. Hainstock, Plume 1997, ISBN: 9780452279094.

A ton of fun stuff that you can do with young kids—autistic and NT—mostly with stuff that's already in your kitchen.

Choosing Home: Deciding to Homeschool with Asperger's Syndrome by Martha Kennedy Hartnett, Jessica Kingsley Publishers 2004, ISBN: 9781843107637.

A personal tale that really opened my eyes to what it might feel like to be a young person with Asperger's trying to navigate the world of teachers and students.

Teaching at Home: A New Approach to Tutoring Children with Autism and Asperger's Syndrome by Olga Holland, Jessica Kingsley Publishers 2005, ISBN: 9781843107873.

This book offers a lot of concrete ideas and helped me to let go of the idea that I was going to personally fix my kid's life by designing the perfect education for her (and, conversely, that I would ruin her life by failing to do That One Perfect Thing, Whatever That Is).

A Slant of Sun: One Child's Courage by Beth Kephart, W.W. Norton & Company 1998, ISBN: 9780688172282.

Both sad and hopeful, this book is a parent's memoir of the confusing, heart-rending, and heart-warming early years with her son, whose diagnosis is PDD-NOS.

Out of Silence: An Autistic Boy's Journey into Language and Communication by Russell Martin, Penguin 1995, ISBN: 9780140247015.

A writer's story about his beloved nephew. The author has done a lot of research, and he brings a journalist's voice to the argument about the causes of and possible remedies for autism.

Look Me in the Eye: My Life with Asperger's by John Elder Robinson, Broadway 2008, ISBN: 9780307396181.

Thank you, John Elder Robison, for blowing the *nom de sibling* that Augustine Burroughs gave to you in *Running with Scissors* and writing this book. A good memoir is like a visit to another country. This one took me to another planet: the planet of the Aspergians. Robison wryly compares himself at various points to a machine, an animal, or an alien, but he is none of these things; he is touchingly human and vulnerable. Diagnosed with Asperger's Syndrome in middle age, Robison finally understood his feats of engineering (he invented KISS's fire-breathing guitars!), as well as his inability to make small talk or to refrain from terrifying pranks.

Deceptively Delicious: Simple Secrets to Get Your Kids Eating Good Food by Jessica Seinfeld, William Morrow 2008, ISBN: 9780061767937.

Yes, I do sneak yam puree into grilled cheese sandwiches. Some days, that might be the only vegetable my kid will eat.

Now, What Do I Do?

1001 Great Ideas for Teaching and Raising Children with Autism Spectrum Disorders by Ellen Notbohm and Veronica Zysk, Future Horizons 2010, ISBN: 9781935274063.

The title does NOT over-promise. Don't even bother putting stickies on the good ideas, because you'll have so many stickies, you'll never find the one you want. Just do all of the stuff on every page!

Breakthrough: New Instructional Approaches to Autism by Karen Sewell, Attainment Company 2008, ISBN: 9781578610600.

Practical advice for parents and teachers.

Toilet Training for Individuals with Autism or other Developmental Issues by Maria Wheeler, M.Ed., Future Horizons 2007, ISBN: 9781932565492.

Just read it. It might help! It helped us.

Maybe It's Autism, Maybe It's Not …

Building Bridges through Sensory Integration: Therapy for Children with Autism and Other Pervasive Developmental Disorders by Paula Aquilla, Shirley Sutton, and Ellen Yack, Future Horizons , ISBN: 9781932565454.

This was the book that was given to me by my dear, gentle friend Tamy when my Grace was still very, very little. She never said the word "autism" (which might, at the time, have scared me), but she pointed me in the direction I needed to go. Sensory differences aren't always indicative of autism, but I am forever in Tamy's debt.

Late Talking Children by Thomas Sowell, Ph.D., Basic Books 1998, ISBN: 9780465038350.

The Einstein Syndrome: Bright Children Who Talk Late by Thomas Sowell, Ph.D., Basic Books 2002, ISBN: 9780465081417.

Is your child socially immature? Late to talk? Late to potty train? These two books might convince you that your child isn't really on the autism spectrum; he's just a plain ol' genius. I would love to hear an update from this author, now that his son is grown and the research has advanced so much. I found these books very thought-provoking.

I also recommend any of the plethora of good books out there on manners, feelings, idioms, and social skills. These are great read-alouds, even if your child can read to himself. There are so many good ones, I hesitate to single any out, but we read *How to Behave and Why* and *Manners Can be Fun* by Munro Leaf over and over again. Sesame Street also has several wonderful books on friendship and social skills, and Carrie Finn has published a set of books with titles like *Manners on the Telephone* and *Manners in the Library*.

And Finally, Something to Think About

Here's a snippet from a new website I found:

"Neurodiversity: Its basic premise is that atypical neurological wiring is part of the normal spectrum of human differences and is to be tolerated and respected like any other human difference ...."

(www.rethinkingautism.com/RethinkingAutism/Key_Concepts.html)

Index

INDEX

About the Authors

Bobbi Sheahan

(What else could you want to know about me?) I left my legal career in 2003 to accept a promotion to full-time mommy and part-time writer. This is my labor of love and my third book. I am married to Ben, the handsome superhero disguised as a brilliant electrical engineer, and we have four children. My writing has also recently appeared in *Bookmarks* magazine, Entrepreneur.com, and Thefreelibrary.com. Dr. DeOrnellas and I also write a column about autism for Andaaztv.com.

It is my privilege to know and to introduce you to Dr. DeOrnellas, and I hope that she is a help to your family. She certainly has been more than a help to mine.

Kathy DeOrnellas, Ph.D.

I met my first child with Asperger's Disorder in 1973. I was a college student working in after-school day care. I did not know what Asperger's Disorder was at that time (nor did anyone else in the U.S.). All I knew was that I had a very quirky new fourth grader who would not quit talking about dinosaurs and could not seem to relate to anyone but me on the playground. It was twenty-five years later that I came to understand more about autism spectrum disorders and began to conduct research in the area of high functioning autism. As an Associate Professor at Texas Woman's University in Denton, I had the privilege of working as Principal Investigator of a large team of students dedicated to working with children and adolescents with high functioning autism spectrum disorder. In the course of this research, we worked with more than sixty children with high functioning ASD with the purpose of determining best practices for evaluating these students. We also became acquainted with their parents and some of their siblings and developed a better understanding of their needs.

My current research is two-pronged. First, I lead a team of students who are in the process of determining the extent that girls with ASDs have appeared in the huge number of research articles that have been published in the last ten years. They are reading each and every article to see how many girls have been included in the studies. My hypothesis is that much of what we know about the symptoms and treatment of ASD is based on research with boys and that few girls participated in these studies. If this turns out to be true, we may be doing girls with ASD a great disservice by basing their treatment on very limited information. Second, I am very interested in helping students with ASD make the transition from high school to college. What do these students need to help them be successful? What can colleges do? What do parents need to do? Stay tuned for more information.

In my private practice, I work with children, adolescents, adults, and parents who are affected by ASD. It was through my private practice that I met Bobbi Sheahan and her wonderful family. When Bobbi approached me about working with her on this book, I was happy to sign on. Many of the families with whom I work are overwhelmed by the process of seeking help for their child(ren). I believe this is the book that I could recommend to them as a source of information and support.

I am married to Ron, who makes it possible for me to teach at a university and manage a private practice. He does this by taking care of everything at home while playing in not one, but two rock bands. I also have a daughter, son-in-law, and beautiful grandson.